Roll Call

ENDORSEMENTS

I have learned over the years that community safety does not happen by accident. It takes dedicated men and women who sacrifice their own wellbeing every day for the cause of others. This service is not just a job, it is a calling that requires a depth of sacrificial giving that cannot be measured.

Roll Call is a pathway to a greater sense of encouragement and peace for all law enforcement officers. It provides a sense of spiritual wellness during difficult and challenging times. My friend, Bobby Kipper, has set the tone for how officers can navigate the trauma they witness every day and still find that strength and inner peace that passes all understanding.

Kevin Malone - Former Vice President and General Manager, Los Angeles Dodgers
Founder and CEO, United States Institute Against Human Trafficking

Very few professions involved the combination of intensity, life-and-death critical decision-making, and expectation of 100% perfection in decision-making and action that law-enforcement officers must face each day. When they put on that badge, it is their duty to respond to the most horrific acts evil, humanity can express toward each other and stand in the gap, to protect the innocent. Their passion to protect and serve often regularly exposes them to trauma, hurt, and losses that many of us will never experience in our lifetime. Front-line community safety takes its toll on these community heroes, oftentimes in unseen ways.

Bobby Kipper's work in *Roll Call* provides today's law enforcement professionals with a much-needed tool to develop a greater sense of peace and anchoring, expanding their self-care from physical, social, and emotional to include spiritual wellness. Their experience in the profession helps them to deliver encouragement and strength from the Bible in a way that is relatable to today's law enforcement community. "Blessed are the peacemakers" (Matt. 5:9). And blessed they will be through *Roll Call*.

Danny Holland, Ph.D., LPC, NCC, BC-TMH, ACS -
Assistant ProfessorTherapist/Former LEO
School of Psychology and Counseling,
Regent University, Virginia Beach, Virginia

Spirituality is an often-overlooked component of total wellness. Religion aside, doing something for the greater good or believing in something greater than yourself improves resiliency and can lead to increased career longevity. This is a much-needed resource and a must-read for officers, wellness program coordinators, and family members.

Katherine Kuhlman. Psy.D. – Public Safety Clinical
Psychologist, Kuhlman Psychology and Counseling

With the focus over the past few years on officer wellness, it's time to focus on a wholistic view and realize that spiritual wellness is an often-forgotten piece of the officer wellness puzzle. I know of very few police officers who haven't felt a comforting "unseen presence" at critical times when performing their duties. *Roll Call: Spiritual Wellness for Today's Law Enforcement Officer* guides an officer and their family through recognition of the unseen presence they have felt but with which they may not have developed a personal relationship. While this book is written from a Christian perspective, hopefully it will serve as the foundation for each law enforcement family to begin their own process of spiritual wellness that could just be the missing link they have been searching for in their quest for total wellness.

Chief Brett Railey (Ret.)
Winter Park Police Department
Past President, Florida Police Chiefs Association

Bobby Kipper's book, *Roll Call: Spiritual Wellness for Today's Law Enforcement Officer,* is timely. As communities all across the nation are calling for police reform, there is also a call to consider the health and wellness of the working law enforcement officer.

Roll Call brings out the deep connection between the teaching and examples from Scripture and the daily encounters and experiences of today's law enforcement professionals. For those officers and deputies who practice their faith and are students of the Bible, this connection will no doubt ring true and provide comfort when the weight of all they see on a regular basis begins to trouble their spirit.

No matter what faith you follow, *Roll Call* can touch your heart. As we know, we are more than just body and mind; we also have a soul, a spiritual side which is impacted by all we experience in life. In this conversation on reform, addressing the spiritual needs of our law enforcement officers is as important as considering their physical and mental health.

When our law enforcement officers have this balance in their lives, the ability to perform their duties in a fair, just, and rational manner will come naturally. Afterall, they got into this job to do the right thing and serve the interests of justice.

Roll Call will offer our working men and women inspirational wisdom from an experienced and seasoned police officer who found in the balance of his spiritual life and his working life the comfort and strength to carry on when it would have been easier to quit.

Jerald Monahan, Chief of Police,
Yavapai College-Prescott, Arizona

The need for spiritual resiliency is critical in the life of a soldier or a police officer. I have reviewed the book *Roll Call* by Kipper, and it certainly fits the bill. Only fellow police officers can really understand the challenges that other officers are facing, especially in the trying times that we are living in. I highly recommend this book and believe that it will cause an officer to dig deep and find real solutions to the challenges that he or she may be facing on the job or in their personal lives. A great read.

Father Michael Pacella III, Author, *From Valor to Virtue*: *The Moral Development of the Brave*

Being a police officer takes a unique person and is a special calling. Those who serve in law enforcement often see people behaving at their worst, and every encounter with the public is potentially a life-threatening situation. How many of us can say this is true about our own occupations on a day-to-day basis?

We must pray for those who serve in law enforcement and encourage them to do their work to the glory of God. *Roll Call* is a book that will help accomplish this. It gives the reader a challenge to pursue Christ and keep him as the center of your life and vocation.

I've known Bobby Kipper for years, and he's the real deal. He loves the Lord, and he has a heart for those who serve in law enforcement. During his time as a police officer, he served the community in which I live with character and excellence. He writes with great insight, respect, and admiration for those who wear the badge. I believe this is an important book, given the challenges police officers are facing these days. If you serve in law enforcement or love someone who does, get this book today.

Wes Taylor – Senior Pastor, Temple Baptist Church, Newport News, Virginia

ROLL CALL

SPIRITUAL WELLNESS FOR
TODAY'S LAW ENFORCEMENT OFFICER

WALL STREET JOURNAL AND USA TODAY BEST SELLING AUTHOR

BOBBY KIPPER

NASHVILLE

NEW YORK • LONDON • MELBOURNE • VANCOUVER

ROLL CALL
SPIRITUAL WELLNESS FOR TODAY'S LAW ENFORCEMENT OFFICER

Published in New York, New York, by Morgan James Publishing. Morgan James is a trademark of Morgan James, LLC. www.MorganJamesPublishing.com

Scripture marked KJV is taken from the King James Version of the Bible, public domain.

ISBN 9781631953606 paperback
ISBN 9781631953613 eBook
Library of Congress Control Number:
2020948154

Cover Design by:
Rachel Lopez
www.r2cdesign.com

Interior Design by:
Chris Treccani
www.3dogcreative.net

Morgan James is a proud partner of Habitat for Humanity Peninsula and Greater Williamsburg. Partners in building since 2006.

Get involved today! Visit
MorganJamesPublishing.com/giving-back

TABLE OF CONTENTS

ACKNOWLEDGMENTS

Special thanks to David Hancock for supporting and understanding the critical need for law enforcement to be given the opportunity to make spiritual wellness a vital part of their support system.

Special thanks to the men and women, past and present, of the Newport News (Virginia) Police Department for allowing us to be part of the family that continues to protect and serve.

Special thanks to Joe St. John for his encouragement in this process.

Special thanks to the saints, past and present, of Temple Baptist Church in Newport News who raised a young child who has had the opportunity to meet and hopefully help people to see the value of a spiritual journey in their daily work.

Special gratitude to the staff at Morgan James Publishing who crafted these words into an awesome offering that we hope will serve as an inspiration to all who read it.

All our thanks to God our Father who blesses us far beyond measure. Let these words be a testament to your mighty grace and love for all who read them.

FOREWORD

It was a beautiful sunrise in Washington, DC. I was taking a walk along the tidal basin to visit the Martin Luther King, Jr. Memorial. I often go there to reflect on Dr. King's example of serving God and mankind by becoming drum majors for love, freedom, justice, and peace. On this particular day, I went to the memorial to reflect on the sad and tragic events that unfolded in our nation with the deaths of Ahmaud Arbery, Breonna Taylor, and George Floyd.

The day after the emotionally charged memorial for George Floyd in Minneapolis, I was seeking inspiration on how to bridge the divide between police and the black community. I was also searching for stepping stones to reconciliation and unity between blacks and whites as the whole world watched how America might achieve social justice while also dealing with the deadly COVID-19 pandemic.

I looked at the various quotes, the statements Dr. King had made in his noble pursuit of building a beloved community. He always aspired to make a seat for everyone at the table of brotherhood. King understood that if we could learn to live together as brothers and sisters, we would not die together due to foolish actions. At the table of brotherhood, we can feast upon the grace and mercy God grants to all of us.

As I approached the memorial, I was surprised to see a large number of police gathered at the site. Initially, I thought they were using the grounds as a staging area to respond to nearby protesters peacefully assembling at Black Lives Matter Plaza near the White House.

However, Police Chief Peter Newsham told me that he wanted to bring new police cadets to the King Memorial for something greater and more thoughtful. He explained that when he watched a Minneapolis police officer put his knee on the neck of George Floyd's neck and keep it there for eight minutes and forty-six seconds, he was deeply troubled: "I was sickened by what I saw with the murder of George Floyd. I was equally sickened by the fact that there were police officers there who didn't stop it from happening."

Newsham further explained his reasons for assembling the police recruits at the MLK Memorial: "The reason that we assembled here today is because we've been watching the things that have been happening across the country with protests and here in Washington too. We're seeing the impact it's having on our police officers. Sometimes people forget that police officers are people too. A lot of the frustration that's out there on what happened to George Floyd is being turned on anyone who wears this uniform, but we're human beings. So, we thought it was really important for command officials to come down here to talk to other police officers. We chose this location because Dr. King is representative of how you affect change in this country."

I watched Sergeant George O'Bryant, a black man who grew up in the area, spend time talking to police cadets about the challenges they would face when they graduated and started serving their communities as police officers. O'Bryant expressed his passion for helping all officers excel in their noble profession of protecting and serving people in their city. He also encouraged them to earn respect, saying, "Just because you have this uniform on, it doesn't always give you respect. You have to have respect in your heart and respect every citizen, every nationality, every race, every community, one at a time."

Sergeant O'Bryant told me the young men and women cadets were part of the police academy and were in the process of training. He looked at them as a proud football coach looks at his team as he told me that he couldn't teach them everything they needed to know. "Some things," he stated, "should have been taught at home while the recruits were growing up. Ninety percent of their training should have come from home. I was brought up in a house where I was taught to respect people, to say, 'Yes, sir,' and 'Yes, ma'am.' We also tell you in the Academy to respect people and say, 'Yes, sir,' and 'Yes, ma'am,' and 'May I help you?' and 'Please.' It's just about respect."

With reflections of George Floyd running through his mind, O'Bryant, with a feeling of remorse in his tone, told me, "It's unfortunate what happened to Mr. Floyd. We watched the video a number of times in the classroom. We are not that officer. That's a very sad situation. These guys know that we will not stand there and watch a police partner do that. We would intervene by telling our partner, who may be feeling a little edgy, to stop. George Floyd said several times, 'I can't breathe, I can't breathe!'"

Turning around and taking in the view of Dr. King's granite statue looking down at us, the sergeant reflected, "We're standing here today, at the MLK Memorial, to recognize a man who fought for justice; he fought for freedom; he fought for equality; and it doesn't make a difference what color you are. We are standing here on what I call solemn ground for a memorial that all of us fought for. The community needs to know that not all officers are bad. We are good officers. Every police officer wants to help the community."

O'Bryant encouraged his fellow officers and cadets to start every day by praying. He told everyone that he has a can of PAM on his desk. He uses that can of PAM to encourage his officers, telling them, "You use PAM to make it non-stick. Yes, people will get frustrated and people will get hurt, but you spray PAM on you—not literally but figuratively—and those problems will not stick."

PAM, he adds, really stands for *Prayer and Meditation*. "That's what we all need every day, no matter who you bow to or kneel to. We all need to pray every day, and that's very important. That's how I start my day. And throughout my day, I might pray for that citizen at an accident scene. I might pray for that victim of child abuse. I might pray for that woman or man who's been sexually assaulted. We have to start off with prayer and meditation to heal. I'll take a knee for that every morning and do it every day. If it wasn't for him, I wouldn't be here."

My visit to the King Memorial was more encouraging than I had anticipated. It provided me a glimpse into the life of a police sergeant and a police chief. I saw how they actively care for their fellow officers in blue and for the people they are called to protect and serve, regardless of the color of their skin. For them, it's about character. They are dedicated to informing and inspiring officers to be ready—mentally, physically, and spiritually—for roll call.

In this book, *Roll Call: Spiritual Wellness for Today's Law Enforcement Officer*, author Bobby Kipper reveals the value of police officers being fully armed with the whole armor of God, not just equipped with a gun and a badge. The authors are aware that in the aftermath of George Floyd there is a great demand for police reform.

Roll Call sets the tone that better reform can take place when all of us will not conform to a culture of division but be transformed by the renewing of our mind. Police and citizens must learn to band together in respecting each other with love, freedom, and peace.

Kelly Wright

Host of *The Kelly Wright Show*, Black News Channel

INTRODUCTION

Police officer, deputy, peace officer, whatever title we were given, it made our chest swell with pride when we received it. We chose the law enforcement profession to make a difference, to make our community a better place to live. We understood that it was our duty to serve.

As time passes, we in the law enforcement profession often forget why we chose this career. After long days, struggles, and apathy, it becomes easy just to go through the motions. We arrest people and see them set free. We observe justice being ignored. We witness more pain and suffering in a week than most people see in a lifetime.

Law enforcement professionals are asked to handle what others choose to ignore. Anyone who has ever carried a badge of authority understands the insanity we deal with daily. However, not everyone sees our problems. Sometimes, even those closest to us—our spouses, children, and friends—do not realize the pressure we work under. They do not see the suffering we have seen. Sometimes, we can't even explain the suffering to them. We grow quiet and distant, not sharing our true feelings.

The job skews our sense of reality. What others see as terrible, we see as routine. What other people call horrible is our daily life. We are the people the community calls when life gets out of control. We are counselors, referees, mediators, doctors, and lawyers. We are asked to give everything we have, and then the people we protect tell us to "get bent" or even worse.

We are loved, feared, hated, idolized, and misunderstood. We are law enforcement. We are often the only people standing in the way of chaos.

But are we really in it alone? Does no one else understand? Luckily, the answer is no. The one who truly understands our situation is Jesus, the risen Lord.

The Son of Man understands the problems we face. He has seen sin and heard the call of the suffering and afflicted. He has paid the price of salvation and is our rock to lean on. He is our solid foundation.

In a world of chaos, we must have a foundation to build on. In a world of confusion, we need a focus and a standard. And what better standard than the living Messiah?

We invite you to explore, over the next several chapters, the challenges facing the law enforcement community today. We will look at the struggles that the men and women in peacekeeping encounter and consider how these struggles can be conquered through Jesus, our conqueror.

We hope the following chapters will help lighten the load for peace officers. We hope that this book gives law enforcement professionals and their families some thoughts to reflect upon and a chance to meditate on the Word of God. Share your reflections from these readings with your family and friends to give them a chance to better understand what we do for a living.

And finally, we hope all readers will realize that we should turn our lives over to the only begotten Son. He understands our situation and has seen our struggles. He is our light and our salvation.

PSALM 23

The LORD is my shepherd; I shall not want.

He maketh me to lie down in green pastures: he leadeth me beside the still waters.

He restoreth my soul: he leadeth me in the paths of righteousness for his name's sake.

Yea, though I walk through the valley of the shadow of death, I will fear no evil: for thou art with me; thy rod and thy staff they comfort me.

Thou preparest a table before me in the presence of mine enemies: thou anointest my head with oil; my cup runneth over.

Surely goodness and mercy shall follow me all the days of my life: and I will dwell in the house of the LORD forever.

CHAPTER 1
THE CALLING

Do you remember how good you felt the first day you put on your uniform? The excitement was unbelievable. You felt like a new person. You may even remember the first time you went out in public and saw the reaction of others. People *did* notice you when in uniform. They *did* treat you differently.

As our careers progress, we may lose some of the thrill. Maybe we look a little more closely at what our career means and see the dirty underbelly of the world. Our attitude may change, and some of those changes are not for the best.

Maybe, at times, we even reassess our profession and goals. As Christians, questions can arise: Are we doing the right thing? Is this what the Lord wants us to do? Are we *really* making a difference?

If you've ever asked these questions, we have good news. Law enforcement can be considered a calling from God, as is clearly stated in Romans 13:1: "Everyone must submit himself to the governing authorities, for there is no authority except that which God has established. The authorities that exist have been established by God." This verse tells us that no authority except that which God has established will ever exist. From the Ten Commandments to modern-day conspiracy laws, it is evident that society will continue to disobey the established law. As society changes, so will the law. But God will always need professional men and women to be ambassadors in the area of law enforcement.

The job is tough and often underappreciated. It has even been said that law enforcement is a career where excellence is not rewarded but expected. It is safe to say that citizens are quick to blame the police for many issues in today's society.

Part of our calling is to continue our mission, not seeking our own fame and fortune but doing good while serving others. A basic Christian principle is to give a helping hand to those in need. It should warm our souls to know that police officers are called to this task twenty-four hours a day, seven days a week, fifty-two weeks a year.

We are up against heavy odds. The media, politicians, and often the public want to make us the scapegoat for society's ills. It becomes increasingly difficult to police a society that has developed such a self-righteous attitude in the midst of wrongdoing. The attitude that it is acceptable to break the law as long as we don't get caught is becoming a way of life in America. Paul touches on this attitude in Romans 13:2 and 13:5: "Consequently, he who rebels against the authority is rebelling against what God has instituted, and those who do so will bring judgment on themselves . . . Therefore, it is necessary to submit to the authorities, not only because of possible punishment, but also because of conscience."

He points out that a person's conscience, not the possibility of punishment, should be the driving force in deciding whether to obey the law. God continues to need men and women who possess the courage to deal with a society that demonstrates a lack of conscience toward their fellow man. It is society's lack of judgment that creates the need for public safety servants.

Bible verses become clearer as we gain more law enforcement experience. Countless people who have been arrested are quick to blame the police for their misfortunes. Yet Paul clearly writes in Romans 13:2 that people who rebel against authority bring judgment on themselves. On more than one occasion, we have shared with citizen groups the fact that the police do not put anyone in jail. People put themselves there.

As our mission grows and we see more and more of the world, we have to be on guard not to make the same mistakes as society. We must always be on guard to do the right thing for the right reason. We need to avoid common pitfalls.

Galatians 5:26 states, "Let us not become conceited, provoking and envying each other." Many law enforcement officers develop big-ego syndrome early in their careers; over time, it can prove to be a serious problem. The power and authority we possess is enormous. With that power comes the risk of conceit. Some officers think they are bigger than life itself. Paul spoke of this attitude in Galatians; he pleads for us not to become conceited. Each of us need a reality check: are you eager to serve your fellow man, or do you choose to build your own image?

"Before his downfall, a man's heart is proud, but humility comes before honor" (Prov. 18:12).

One of the proudest moments of our lives was the day we graduated from the police academy. We had finally accomplished our lifelong dream of becoming a police officer. We were decked out in our uniforms, feeling like we could take on the world. That was such a great feeling, and anyone in that position has the right to be proud. Proud moments are good for self-esteem, but to live constantly in pride is dangerous. Proverbs 18 clearly points out the destructive nature of pride. Remember a proud moment but beware a proud heart.

At times, you may develop a sense of being Superman while doing police work. You will find that battered women see you as their knight in shining armor. Victims of sexual and child abuse see you as a sort of miracle worker. While you may appear to be many different things for many different people, always remember you are human, and you do have faults and personal issues of your own. We all need to experience a certain amount of humility to stay in touch with our true selves.

To make sure we stay focused, it is important to assess our behaviors. Are we acting in a way that would make our parents, families, and departments proud? Are we doing all the right things for the right reasons? Consider the words of Psalm 37:16: "Better the little that the righteous have than the wealth of the many wicked."

Have you ever had the feeling as a law enforcement officer that you are underpaid? At some point in your career, you will compare your salary to the corporate world. It stirs even more discontent when we see people prosper because of their involvement in criminal activity. Psalm 37 clears a path for us to see that the righteous may have little, but compared to the wicked, they are fortunate. We have to continue to trust God, and he will see that our needs are met.

The Lord has a special place for all who choose to bring justice to a confused world. The Bible teaches that all have sinned. As police officers, we certainly see the darkness of the world. If we acknowledge God's power, he will honor us in a special way. The psalmist also believed this when he lifted up in praise a blessing to those who maintain justice:

> *"Blessed are they who maintain justice, who constantly do what is right" (Ps. 106:3).*

> *"Righteousness guards the man of integrity, but wickedness overthrows the sinner" (Prov. 13:6).*

The cornerstone of a law enforcement officer is integrity. Without integrity, you will be doomed in this profession. Some years ago, we learned that a number of officers in our department had been frequenting a local sports bar. The problem was that the owner of this bar was a known sports bookie. While it was difficult to prove that our police officers were betting on sporting events, it had the overall appearance of impropriety. Police officers should be on guard at all times concerning the issue of integrity. While many officers may not intend to present a questionable image, we must keep in mind that, as law enforcement officers, our actions are closely watched.

Police corruption is one of the most dangerous areas we experience as an occupation. Raising a hand in pledge to accept the public trust, we are promising to never deny the honor and dignity of our called profession. Yet, throughout America each and every day, some police officers choose deceit over dignity. One blemish on law enforcement causes months and years of damage in the public eye to those of us who seek to do what is right. When an officer chooses the wrong road, they place all of us in a negative light. While none of us are perfect, we all realize the difference between what is honorable and what is tarnished behavior. Let us stand for what is right, now and always. Remember the words of Exodus 23:8: "Do not accept a bribe, for a bribe blinds those who see and twists the words of the righteous."

As police officers, we must understand that the core of justice remains in our ability to be impartial. It will be difficult to perform the tasks we face if we show partiality. People have great difficulty understanding when public servants treat individuals differently. Justice depends on our ability to enforce the law equally. Realistically, this does not happen in all cases, but it should be our goal to make it happen.

We must always keep our guard up to those who would attempt to lead us down the path of destruction. Good character and credibility are two important characteristics of a law enforcement officer. We must wisely choose our friends so that they will understand the importance of our maintaining our good name. Police corruption is still a problem in today's society. The police officer on "the take," unfortunately, is not a thing of the past. Just as Paul challenged the church at Corinth, we must also answer his challenge to be free from corruption. With God's help and our willingness to ask for it, we can overcome this dangerous temptation.

> *"Do not be overcome by evil but overcome evil with good"*
> *(Rom. 12:21).*

We constantly are surrounded by the products of evil. It is the nature of our profession. We have witnessed evil change the lives of some police officers—and definitely not for the better. We must always be on guard not to let the darkness we witness control our own lives. The best advice in this area would be not to let your job shape your personality but to let your personality shape the job you do. The power of the risen Lord is there for you if you choose to use it.

One of the hardest temptations for people to overcome is that of seeking revenge. Law enforcement officers see so many innocent people victimized that it becomes easy for us to wish hard times on those who commit crimes against the innocent. But the Bible teaches against trading evil for evil. Even though it may be difficult, we need to concentrate on wanting the best for everyone. Jesus served as a great example when he asked the Lord to forgive those who were putting him on the cross. If Jesus could forgive those who tormented him, we, too, can forgive those who commit evil.

The concept of forgiveness is easy to forget as the world around us operates in a revenge mode. People feel that when someone has committed a wrong against them, they have the right to strike back. As law enforcement officers who seek justice, we cannot afford to operate on this basis. At times, we all want to see what many call "street justice," but we must admit this attitude is truly wrong. Our job is to right what is wrong, not to continue on a path that leads to revenge. True justice will happen, but we need to wait for God's timing, not our own.

When you think of all the difficulties we face, it is amazing what we accomplish. But God has given us his word that we will be victorious: "Do you not know that in a race all the runners run, but only one gets the prize? Run in such a way as to get the prize" (1 Cor. 9:24).

Today's demands continue to grow on law enforcement officers throughout America. This is not an occupation that allows for a slack work ethic. We are constantly under the gun to serve as role models and produce results. Some officers may remember a time when you could go an entire shift with very few calls. In most cities today, however, low call volume is a rare occurrence. Law enforcement is demanding by the very nature of our responsibility. We are constantly called to intervene in highly stressful situations that demand our full attention and stamina. How do we accomplish these feats? We must "look to the Lord and his strength; seek his face always" (Ps. 105:4).

As law enforcement officers, we are trained to depend on various weapons for self-defense. When we carry a firearm in the community, it gives us that extra feeling of protection. Issues within the last several years have placed a real burden on the use-of-force policies in most departments. We also face the constant outcry from citizens who complain about police overreacting in certain situations. All of this certainly does not make our job easier. Do not just arm yourself physically. Arm yourself with scripture, and all things will become clear.

The job of law enforcement brings with it a great deal of hardship. Tough hours, poor working conditions, and low pay are just a few of the problems we deal with on a regular basis. At times, it would be easy to look at our hardship as punishment, but the Bible encourages us to look on hardship as discipline. This perspective may be difficult to hold when you are in the midst of a problem or a tough situation, but it is the correct answer.

As a law enforcement officer, you may never win a popularity contest. Some people in our society have a problem with police officers. They may dislike you simply for what you stand for: authority. The world needs correction and direction, but most would not admit it. Jesus spoke about what to expect in the world: "If the world hates you, keep in mind that it hated me first" (John 15:18). His words indicate that when we are hated for righteousness' sake, he identifies with our pain. Jesus paid the supreme price for standing for what was good and proper. He was crucified an innocent man so that we could inherit eternal life.

As public safety officers, we are constantly placed in positions of danger. Each year in America, we lose a number of law enforcement officers to sudden, tragic death. These brave men and women have given their all for the cause of personal freedom for all citizens. As law enforcement officers, we experience a deep personal loss at the slaying of a fellow officer. It is a difficult feeling to get over. Jesus had special words to share about those who would sacrifice their lives for other people. His words should be a blessing: "Greater love has no one than this, that he lay down his life for his friends" (John 15:13). I can't help but think that our fallen comrades will have a special place in the kingdom.

Is law enforcement a calling? We think so, as our profession is one of the most important in society and is ordained by God. What makes a good police officer? That question has been asked numerous times. As society has changed so have the requirements of what type of person will succeed in law enforcement. In the past, law enforcement attracted individuals who served fellow citizens from their heart and with a true desire. Today's society requires a great deal of patience and self-control from those called to the field of law enforcement. In Galatians 5:22-23, Paul talks about the fruit of the spirit: "But the fruit of the Spirit is love, joy, peace, patience, kindness, goodness, faithfulness, gentleness, and self-control." As you read this verse, compare the characteristics in this passage to the personal qualities needed to succeed in law enforcement or any other professional occupation.

CHAPTER REFLECTIONS

- Law enforcement can be a calling, God's chosen field for you.
- A man's conscience is a blueprint of his character.
- To serve others is our calling, even if it means we must deny ourselves.
- When choosing between righteousness and riches, always choose the first.
- Don't let your job shape your personality; let your personality shape the job you do.
- Run the race in such a way as to win the prize.
- Evil will pay the same dividends as revenge.
- Look to the Lord and his strength.
- Remember, you are blessed.
- Seize a proud moment but live with humility.

PRAYER FOR THE CALLING

God, show me your will for my life as I choose to be of service to you and my fellow man in the area of law enforcement. Spread your wisdom to those who would consider rebelling against the recognized authority. Help them to resist and turn from the darkness and to recognize truly that all authority is given through you. Give me a pure heart, a bold faith, and a clear conscience. Give me a heart that is right for service to others. Help me to concentrate on my calling and keep my heart from conceit. Keep me on task to serve others.

Let me trust you for my needs. Help me to seek your will and lean on you in a materialistic world. Protect me from the darkness, deliver me from evil, and guide me toward your great light. I pray for strength in my duties and responsibilities. Give me the energy to carry on in a world that is draining. Lead me on a path that is pure and true to your calling. Let me honor what is right and, most of all, do what is pleasing in your sight. Teach me to be patient and not to encourage revenge. I rest on your promise that evil deeds will be called to task and that your grace will protect all who believe and seek your ways. Forgive me when I succumb to the misuse of my position to gain favor from man rather than from you. Amen.

CHAPTER 2
THE BEATITUDES OF THE BEAT ATTITUDES

Every one of us is familiar with Jesus's Sermon on the Mount. We have heard about it in Sunday school and seen it in plays and film. But have you ever thought about the words Jesus spoke? They are incredible in that they contradict everything we've been taught. The weak are strong? Mourning is a blessing? How can this be true?

In the Kingdom of God, everything is judged differently. God is calling us to be light in the world. Jesus came and offered himself a sacrifice. The greatest man ever to be born did not come to rule the world but to save it. Even as Christ hung on the cross, he was mocked: "Likewise, also the chief priests mocking said among themselves with the scribes, He saved others; himself he cannot save" (Mark 15:31).

Even in the last moments of his life, Jesus heard people questioning the Kingdom of God. They were mocking him, laughing at his impending death. They did not understand that out of the shame of the cross, the glory of the resurrection would be created. They did not understand that out of the weakness of death, the power of everlasting life would be born.

The chief priests had been blinded by the world. They mistook strength for power and forgot that God's rules are not the rules of the world. They forgot the power of the almighty God.

The Beatitudes are one of the greatest sermons ever written. They explain the Kingdom of God and describe the world ordained by God. They are words as useful today as when they were spoken two thousand years ago and should still rule our lives. They are not just Jesus's Beatitudes but they should also be our Beat Attitudes.

During the remainder of this chapter, we will explore the richness of Jesus's words. Are they relevant today? Are we confusing the world's ideas with God's? Do we have the proper Beat Attitudes?

"Blessed are the poor in spirit, for theirs is the kingdom of heaven" (Matt. 5:3).

During our tour of duty, we may come upon people in need of food, clothing, or shelter. The first time we experience this revelation, we may wonder how people live in this way. In addition, we may ask ourselves if this is our problem. The poor and hungry are everyone's problem. While we may not be able to supply all of the needs of the people we meet, we can constantly try to link them to other community resources. Is there a food bank in your town you could refer them to? While some people are lacking for material items, they are still open to God's blessings. The Bible does not measure our stake in the kingdom by our earthly riches. We are all judged according to our faith, not our equity.

> *"Blessed are those who mourn, for they will be comforted"*
> *(Matt. 5:4).*

When was the last time you witnessed an officer of the law mourn? Have you ever had to witness a law enforcement officer's funeral? It is truly one of the saddest days that peace officers will ever experience. When a law enforcement officer is murdered, a little part of each of us also dies. The wind blows a little colder. And the sky is a little darker. The sadness that comes from this event is a reminder of the suffering that exists in the world. It is a reminder that nothing in life is certain.

Officers will travel for miles to pay respect to a fallen comrade. They will honor the slain officer with a black ribbon or a covered badge. We mourn the loss of an officer like a family member because we are a family.

Jesus mourns with us. He understands the sadness that we feel. He feels it too. That is why we are blessed when we mourn. We are blessed because we feel the same way our Lord feels about suffering. We are blessed in sharing the same suffering as the Savior.

To mourn does not necessarily mean to weep openly. At times, we mourn in our heart while not shedding a tear. Police officers, for a number of reasons, are afraid to show their true emotions. God will comfort your inner heart and instill hope to your soul. Remember, Jesus said that mourning is a blessing, so feel free to share your emotions. We share them with our Savior.

"Blessed are the meek, for they will inherit the earth" (Matt. 5:5).

Most law enforcement officers have a special place in their heart for the elderly. It is always sad for us to see an elderly person who has been swindled out of his or her life's earnings by a thief. Sadly, we have people who choose to thrive on the meek in our society. We have always attempted to provide safety and security to the meek. We should find comfort in the fact that we are called to protect the meek, for they depend on us.

We are equally pulled toward the young. When we see an infant who has been hurt, we feel the need to protect the innocent. Officers who can stomach the worst car accidents are often upset about the death of a child. Murders occur often, and we sometimes fail to notice, until a child is the victim.

Our call to protect the meek is essential. It is necessary. Jesus promised to protect the meek. He said, "[The meek] will inherit the earth."

"Blessed are those who hunger and thirst for righteousness, for they will be filled" (Matt. 5:6).

We may feel, at times, that much of the world is attracted to crime and evil. We must always keep in mind that most people are good, decent, and law-abiding citizens. One problem that we face is that righteous deeds performed every day are overshadowed by the evil around us. Much of this is due to the constant media coverage of crime and violence. Always remember that the righteous are out there, even if our job does not highlight their presence. The Bible encourages us to hunger and thirst for righteousness, but more important, it promises that our hunger will be filled.

"Blessed are the merciful, for they will be shown mercy"
(Matt. 5:7).

How much mercy can you show in your job as a law enforcement officer? You'll face decisions about whether to take a person to court or not. We like to call it discretion. Many departments do not like their officers to have a great deal of discretion, but it will always remain part of our job. No one expects a law enforcement officer to look the other way when someone is committing a serious violation of the law. But in plenty of instances in the course of your duties, you will be able to show a form of mercy. Resisting the use of force when it is appropriate and letting a judge know that your defendant was cooperative are just a couple of ways you can show mercy.

"Blessed are the pure in heart, for they will see God"
(Matt. 5:8).

What is our motive for serving others? This question is one we should focus on daily. This issue is not one that will be addressed through job-related evaluation; rather, it must be checked through self-evaluation. While others may not know our motives or intentions, we need to ensure that our actions are above reproach. Many law enforcement officers run into problems when they lose focus. Keeping our hearts in the right place is not easy. If we only lean on our own strength, it may be impossible, but with God's help, anything is possible.

"Blessed are the peacemakers, for they will be called sons of God" (Matt. 5:9).

We will all agree that violence never solved anything. From domestic violence to street violence, no one wins when people choose war over reason. Every violent act creates a victim. People's lives are changed in the face of violence. As police officers, we should lead society as peacemakers. We should serve as role models in the area of conflict mediation. We can show others how to keep their heads in the face of adversity. Remember, the ability to keep your cool is not always easy. Some of the citizens you meet will find a way to push your buttons. When it comes to keeping our cool, we live in a house of glass. How will you respond in the face of conflict?

"Blessed are those who are persecuted because of righteousness, for theirs is the kingdom of heaven" (Matt. 5:10).

No other occupation in America creates the atmosphere for persecution like law enforcement. Because we serve every day in a recognized uniform and drive a marked vehicle, we are wide open to public scrutiny. Each and every day, law enforcement officers throughout America are falsely accused of brutality and other job-related complaints. It seems that we spend a great deal of time living in glass houses. While we may feel a lack of respect coming from certain people in our society, it is always important to remember that God will reward those who are persecuted for righteousness' sake.

> *"Blessed are you when people insult you, persecute you and falsely say all kinds of evil against you because of me"* (Matt. 5:11).

Do you remember the first time you heard a pig-type noise or an insult to announce your presence? Is it hurtful that we go out daily and lay our life on the line only to be insulted? It is important to learn what all law enforcement officers need to know: we cannot take the insults we receive personally. You will come into contact with people who dislike you for what you represent. Remember, we represent what is good and right. So, even when the insults come, hold your head up and carry on.

> *"Rejoice and be glad, because great is your reward in heaven, for in the same way they persecuted the prophets that were before you"* (Matt. 5:12).

The ability to be glad becomes increasingly important the longer we remain in the law enforcement arena. If we do not guard ourselves, it is easy to develop a critical attitude toward society. Many surveys indicate that the longer people stay in this job, the more cynical they become. If we guard our hearts and ask for help from above, we can be glad instead of jaded.

The Beat Attitudes: are you ready for them? You should be. It is what God is calling all of us to do.

CHAPTER REFLECTIONS

- Mourning may never result in crying.
- We should seek to protect the meek.
- While much attention is given to evil, the righteous keep on moving toward God.
- Mercy shown is mercy earned.
- True victory lies in the face of peace.
- God recognizes those who are persecuted for his sake.
- Attitudes can limit a person's altitude.

PRAYER FOR THE BEAT ATTITUDES

Lord, thank you for your blessings on the poor. Thank you for listening to everyone who calls your name. Comfort my heart. Allow me to experience mourning with the promise that you are our comfort and strength. Bless the meek and lead me to their path so that I may provide a service for you. Keep us hungry for your righteousness. Thank you for your promise to fill us for your service.

Help me to show mercy and grant me the direction to seek your mercy. Protect my heart. Keep it pure and guide my intentions in the right direction. Teach me to be a peacemaker. Guide me in my efforts to lead others to solve their problems without violence. Help me when I am persecuted. Shine your light on me so that I may feel your strength. Protect me from those around me who speak evil toward you. Keep me focused for your sake. Amen.

CHAPTER 3
AND JUSTICE FOR ALL

Have you ever thought about the word *justice* and what it means to you? Have you ever considered how justice impacts society? One man's justice can be another man's injustice. Many people have taken justice into their own hands. We've all seen a case or read about a situation where someone harms another because they felt they had been slighted. Were their actions justice or vengeance?

The Merriam-Webster Dictionary defines *justice* as follows:

> *The maintenance or administration of what is just, especially by the impartial adjustment of conflicting claims or the assignment of merited rewards or punishments, the administration of law; especially:*

the establishment or determination of rights accord-ing to the rules of law or equity, the quality of being just, impartial, or fair, the principle or ideal of just dealing or right action, conformity to this principle or ideal, the quality of conforming to law, conformity to truth, fact, or reason.

We hold high expectations for justice. The above definition uses the lofty words, the very type we expect in explaining the word *justice*. But is justice always served? Are the wrongs of society always corrected? Can we in law enforcement say that justice is always the end result, or do we know better?

Many of us in the law enforcement community have problems with this concept. We arrest people just to see them turned free by the court system. It can be frustrating. Law enforcement officers have no trouble with Justice being blind; it is when we realize she is also deaf and dumb that we get concerned.

It is during these times of concern that we must keep focused on our true mission, the mission of justice. Our goal should be to administer the law justly, without prejudice. We should strive every day to treat everyone, regardless of their status, the same. Law enforcement officers should be above making judgments based on feelings and preconceived thoughts.

We should be making judgments based on the laws we have been sworn to uphold. The law should be our guideline, not whether we like the court system. We are called to be above the fray, a level above the norm.

This calling is not only from our departments but from our God. God is just. In the Bible, the concept of justice is a recurring theme. It is an important factor in all of God's work.

The psalmist wrote, "The Lord works righteousness and justice for all the oppressed" (Ps. 103:6). It is important to remember that we are not alone in our desire for justice. It is important that we feel compassion for those we meet who have been victimized. We want to meet them with humility, right where they are. It is nearly impossible to assist someone when they suspect that the person trying to help them is not sincere.

A sixteen-year-old girl who had been involved in an accident was standing beside the road, hysterical. She was crying, and all she could say, over and over again, was that her dad was going to be mad because she had wrecked the car. Everyone on the scene attempted to calm her down. Her boyfriend and his brother, who had been in the car, were telling her that everything was going to be all right. Police officers arrived, and she was still upset. Finally, her family and her boyfriend's family arrived.

When the girl saw her father, she became more upset, saying she was sorry and had not intended to wreck his car. Police were finally able to talk to the father, who calmed the young lady down. The police officer working the accident scene had the young lady and the other driver make statements, and the officer investigated the accident. When the officer concluded her investigation, it was the other driver who was given a ticket. It had not been the young girl's fault. But it wasn't until she was able to talk to her father and understand that she was not in trouble that she calmed down. The accident was caused by the other driver, but this young lady did not care. She was more concerned that she would get in trouble with her father.

What would have happened if the officer had just responded to the girl's crying? Would justice have been served? What if the officer just took the first statement the sixteen-year-old made about the accident? Would that officer have been fair?

It is comforting to know that the Lord works for justice for all those who are oppressed. We should too. Take your time in assessing situations. Do not jump to conclusions. It is important to understand the victim's point of view.

The prophet Isaiah wrote, "For I, the Lord, love justice; I hate robbery and iniquity. In my faithfulness I will reward them and make an everlasting covenant with them" (Is. 61:8). The world continues to believe, in many ways, that crime pays. This attitude means that many do not fear committing a crime; rather, they fear getting caught.

Throughout Scripture, we see God's way is that of justice. If ever his love of justice is in question, refer to this verse from Isaiah. The beginning words indicate that the Lord loves justice. As we serve to protect justice, it is comforting to know that what we seek is supported by God. As we serve our fellow man, let us open our hearts to also serve the Lord.

The world of drugs has opened a Pandora's box of issues. In many neighborhoods, the bread winner of the household may be a drug dealer. The main income of the household may come from drug profits. Some kids know that the money in their pockets came from the drug trade. Their families have condoned these actions and legitimized drug use in their household.

We live in a society close to saying that drug use is alright. We pray that the law enforcement community never embraces this idea. It is impossible to work in this profession and not see the destruction drugs have caused in our communities. The loss of life is staggering.

The destruction of the family and the murder of innocent people cannot be fully described. Drugs are not a victimless crime. They destroy communities, one individual at a time. Drugs know no sorrow and have no mercy. They are the great equalizer, destroying rich, poor, man, and woman. Drug culture has no heart.

On September 11, 2001, this country suffered one of the saddest days in our history. Thousands of innocent people were murdered, and our country went into mourning. The world, for Americans, had stopped cold. We were no longer innocent; we understood that we were part of a global community teetering on disaster.

People walked through the day as if it were a bad dream. Everywhere you went, the bombing was the only thing people could talk about. The horror was undeniable. The suffering was deep.

In Newport News, all police personnel were called back to duty. We have a large military population, and the police department was on high alert. During the course of the day, numerous meetings were held between military and police personnel. The entire city was at a standstill. It was like nothing anyone had ever seen before.

Even calls for service stopped. It felt like the whole world had shut down. That was until about eleven o'clock that night. An alert tone came over the radio, and officers were advised that a shooting had just occurred. At a local intersection, a man had been shot while riding his moped. When officers arrived, the man was lying face down in his own blood. He was still on top of his moped. Hundreds of screaming people lined the streets. Family members were crying. Some had even brought their children out to watch the spectacle. The news media arrived, and it looked like a sick television show.

It was September 11th. The whole world had stopped to mourn, except for the drug dealers. For them, it was business as usual. Someone had not paid their debts, and the drug lords administered their own justice—death. It was obvious they did not care what day it was.

After witnessing these events, would it be okay to tell someone drugs are acceptable? Would justice be served if we acted like these illegal activities didn't matter? Is the price of death worth the little gain drug sales bring?

How do we in law enforcement battle these problems? The answers are not easy, but they are there. Isaiah was warning the people of Israel that justice was more important than gain—a tough idea for some to understand. Often people want to believe that the end justifies the means. This is not true. It is important that everyone understands we must answer to a greater judge than society.

"Do not be deceived: God cannot be mocked. A man reaps what he sows" (Gal. 6:7).

Police officers may spend many hours preparing solid cases that are eventually set aside by a judge or jury in court. For a critical case, it becomes difficult not to take this matter personally. We must remain focused on bringing those who have violated the written law into the review of the court. Let us never forget that the final judge of human behavior is not swayed by the lawyer for the defense but by the heart of the guilty.

Every day, through our manner and words, we should set an example of understanding God's justice. We have to show that it is more important to be right for the right reason than to have personal gain. The world tells people that as long as they have material things, they will be satisfied.

We need to set the example that God's way is the right way. Also, we should not take it upon ourselves to be the beginning and end of justice. We need to remember that we are merely tools in the system. We are there to be used by God so that justice can prevail.

"When justice is done, it brings joy to the righteous, but terror to evildoers" (Prov. 21:15).

Victory comes when a law enforcement officer successfully testifies in a big case in court. While our hopes are that people would obey the law, it is comforting to see justice prevail when someone chooses to commit a crime. While we should not celebrate outwardly when a suspect is sentenced, it is perfectly natural to feel a sense of accomplishment. The Bible is clear that all who would choose to break the law will one day stand to face the consequences of their actions. It is also important to remember that all things are done for the glory of Jesus Christ and not for our own accomplishments.

"For there is nothing hidden that will not be disclosed, and nothing concealed that will not be known or brought out into the open" (Luke 8:17).

Every city or town has an element of organized criminal activity, but the perpetrators never seem to get caught. A major component of the illegal drug trade in America is the laundering of money by people within our communities. Some of these citizens would have us believe that they are perfect role models. Can they continue to get away with their criminal involvement? Luke 8:17 lets us know that nothing we do will remain hidden. They may hide their actions from man but not from God. Do not worry that the only people concerned about righteousness are the police. In Romans 14:12, it is written, "Each of us will give an account of himself to God."

The world continues to play the blame game when it comes to crime and evil. In law enforcement, we are met with overwhelming resistance when we charge a citizen with a law violation. Think about it. When was the last time you arrested someone who agreed with the charges? The world is bent on denial when it comes to dealing with the law. It is reassuring to know that, according to God's Word, we do not have to worry about this. Romans 14:12 tells us that everyone will be accountable to God for himself and his own actions. That is a court date none of us will escape.

We must understand our responsibility in our communities. We are there to serve and protect. The job is easy when we are talking about people you like. But how about people you don't like? What about the murdered drug dealer? Does he (and his family) deserve justice? The answer has to be yes. We are sworn to protect the whole community, not just the part of the community we like. We are called to be above judgment and to make our decisions based on doing what we are sworn to do: to protect and serve.

The Apostle Paul knew a great deal about public service. He was a great motivator to all public service providers. In Romans 15:1 he writes that those who are strong and righteous in the calling of God should serve to those who are weak or misdirected: "We who are strong ought to bear with the failings of the weak and not to please ourselves." Police officers have traditionally represented strength and truth. We must let the words of the Apostle Paul become our call to action for the poor, the lonely, and the misguided.

Law enforcement officers will always be in demand. God's Word teaches that all mankind is born into sin. As descendants of Adam, we are drawn to that which will separate us from God. The Bible teaches that we need to acknowledge our wickedness and turn to God for cleansing. Scripture explains the deep issue of sin against God, which is not only through our own deeds but those of our fathers as well. Therefore, as police officers, we have certain job security, but as individuals, we must turn to God to be cleansed of our own wrongdoing.

We must be on guard to stay focused on our job. It is easy to get swayed when we see so much that is wrong. We have to be cognizant of the world but not fall prey to its temptations.

If we do not follow the right path, we could be on the path to destruction. An officer who had committed many years of his life to our profession made this mistake and paid a terrible price. The officer faced many of the problems we face every day. He was overworked, tired, and had many financial problems. He had been a good officer during his career, but he could not get ahead.

As time progressed, his problems grew. Finally, he made a deal with some old friends that he would help transport drugs to and from Florida. He would even place his police uniform in the back of the vehicle to ensure that, if he were stopped, he would get the privileges he believed a police officer should receive.

He did this for his friends on a couple of occasions. Finally, in an unrelated incident, one of his friends was arrested. He turned on the police officer and told what he had been doing. The officer was investigated and arrested. He lost his job and was incarcerated. He lost everything he had worked for. He compromised his values and lost his focus because of his problems. He stopped being a police officer and became a criminal.

Different versions of this story occur throughout our country; it's sad but true. And these officers give everyone in the profession a black eye. They make everyone pay for their mistakes. Their lack of focus makes everyone's job in law enforcement more difficult.

We often hear about the police officer who forgets his duty. The same media that wouldn't spend five minutes talking about a positive police story will spend weeks doing an exposé on police corruption. Many media outlets do not want to print the feel-good, soft story of a dedicated police officer, but they will jump at the chance to point out our mistakes and paint the profession with a large brush.

Stay focused on your duties because the psalmist tells us, "Great peace have they who love your law, and nothing can make them stumble" (Ps. 119:165). Do you ever think of the law as a road to peace? Living a life according to the law can be rewarding in many ways, including peace for those who follow it. In contrast, those who choose to live outside of the law should fear the consequences that await them in this world and the next. But for those who follow the rules, life is calm and peaceful. We don't have to look over our shoulder to wonder if we are going to get caught for some violation or wrongdoing. Those who love God's law and choose to live by it have a firm foundation. Nothing can make them stumble.

Do not focus on those who do not like us or appreciate us. Jesus said, "But I tell you: Love your enemies and pray for those who persecute you" (Matt. 5:44). Have you made any enemies lately? We have a job in law enforcement that causes certain people to dislike us. It is interesting that many of these people don't even know us personally. Matthew 5:44 offers some of the toughest advice in the Bible. We are challenged to love our enemies and, even further, to pray for those who persecute us. In a world driven by greed, jealousy, and hate, this admonition may feel tough to do. If we depend on our own strength, it may be impossible to do. That's where God's strength comes into play. We must give our thoughts of revenge and dislike to him. He alone can change our attitude from mad to glad. It is his grace.

Be prepared for what lies ahead. Do not make everything personal. Do not think that everything said about you is really about you. Often, people do not like us for *what* we are, not *who* we are. They know we have authority and stand for justice. Some people find these qualities unacceptable. Everyone who has been involved in law enforcement knows we are the only thing that stands between order and chaos. Those who love chaos hate us. We need to understand that concept and be prepared: "Put on the full armor of God, so that you can take your stand against the devil's schemes" (Eph. 6:11).

Law enforcement officers in today's society can count their blessings for the invention of body armor that protects us from deadly harm. One of the leading manufacturers of this equipment had an apt name: Second Chance. Countless officers would have lost their lives if not for this valuable equipment. Paul speaks to us in the book of Ephesians about a different kind of armor. God's armor gives us a second chance at spiritual life. It protects us, sustains us, and adds abundance to our lives. It helps us take our stand against the devil's schemes. In our position as law enforcement officers, we could sure use the help.

Paul instructs us to be ready for the challenge:

Put on the whole armor of God, that ye may be able to stand against the wiles of the devil. For we wrestle not against flesh and blood, but against principalities, against powers, against the rulers of the darkness of this world, against spiritual wickedness in high places. Wherefore take unto you the whole armor of God, that ye may be able to withstand in the evil day, and having done all, to stand. Stand therefore, having your loins girt about with truth, and having on the breastplate of righteousness; And your feet shod with the preparation of the gospel of peace; Above all, taking the shield of faith, wherewith ye shall be able

to quench all the fiery darts of the wicked. And take
the helmet of salvation, and the sword of the Spirit,
which is the word of God (Eph. 6:11-17).

Paul warns us that our battles are not just with flesh and blood. We are up against higher powers that can only be confronted by a prepared soldier. Read the passage from Ephesians again. Paul does not say, "Hey, just do *your* best and try to stay focused." He doesn't say, "Think positive, and everything will work out." He gives us direct instructions: "Take the whole armor of God; have your loins girded with truth; wear the breast plate of righteousness; wear the gospel of peace; and, above all, take the shield of faith, the helmet of salvation, and the sword of the spirit, the Word of God."

He is instructing us to be prepared. It is not enough to say that I am prepared because I have gone to a law enforcement academy or have had great training. We are up against more than police training alone can handle. We will face thousands and thousands of situations that are never addressed at the academy.

How can we be prepared for these decisions? Paul gives us the answer: follow Scripture and understand your role in the Kingdom of God. Do not back down from the evil ones. Practice the gospel.

Another important message to understand is compassion. The psalmist sang, "As a father has compassion on his children, so the Lord has compassion on those who fear him" (Ps. 103:13). When we first became officers or deputies, we may not have realized the level of compassion that this job would ask. Little did we know that we would witness individuals and families in their darkest hours. An officer who responds to his first infant death call can forever recall the pleas of a mother who lost her only child. None of the training offered at the police academy will help in this situation. It is a heart of compassion that must become our driving force. God has compassion for all people, and he expects us to follow his example. It has been said that the mark of a man is the compassion he shows.

The title of this chapter is "And Justice for All." It is a nice phrase, but it should also be our reality. Take the time to read the following reflections and pray about them. Justice is not a long-lost concept. It should be our goal every day. We should strive to follow justice and have mercy because justice without mercy is not justice at all.

CHAPTER REFLECTIONS

- True acquittal will only come from the one true judge.
- Justice for all is a promise from God; we must wait on his timing.
- The Lord loves justice and hates robbery and iniquity.
- To judge others puts us in a position to be judged.
- Justice means joy to the righteous and terror to the evildoer.
- Nothing is hidden from God.
- Each of us will have to give an account to God.
- The Lord is the Author of Justice.

PRAYER FOR JUSTICE

Lord, please help me understand the source of true justice. Thank you for being the one who controls true justice. Guide me in my daily attempts to serve you and my fellow man. I seek justice for all in a world that has lost its focus. Give me an understanding of true justice, which can only come from you.

Lord, I seek your justice, not that which the world knows, for your justice frees us from all bondage. Help me stay away from the attitude of judging others; let me lean on your grace and look at others as you would have me see them. Amen.

CHAPTER 4
SOCIETY IN NEED

Jesus is the light to redeem the world. He is the answer to the problems of our society. The cost of sin can be seen everywhere. Sin destroys everything in its path. It leads intelligent people into a life of corruption and makes people do things they swore they would never do.

Jesus understands the problem of sin. He made it a point to be with sinners. He was even criticized for these activities. The religious leaders wondered why a man of God would fraternize with prostitutes, tax collectors, and pagans. They thought that a man of God would want to be with the pure, the holy, and the clean. Jesus mystified them.

He made claims of deity and spoke of the law with authority. He also socialized with the less fortunate and with sinners. He came to be their salvation and was aware of his role. When Jesus heard his critics, he had an answer: "It is not the healthy who need a doctor, but the sick I have not come to call the righteous, but sinners" (Mark 2:17).

What an idea! A redemptive God! The religious leaders of the day were shocked. They must have thought the Messiah would run to their doors and honor them for their good works. They may have envisioned the Christ taking them before the synagogues and telling the other Jews how great they were, reciting long lists of their great deeds. What a shock that the Son of Man went to the lost and broken instead.

No parades, no talk of religious greatness occurred. Rather, a simple man with a simple plan of salvation showed up. Religious leaders of the day must have been furious. All that hard work and all they received was rebuke. God's Kingdom came to those *he* chose.

If the Messiah came to twenty-first century America instead of first century Palestine, where would he choose to speak? Would he go to the upscale communities or to the needy? Would he tell everyone how great the church was, or would he expose our weaknesses? Would the beggar and the homeless get more attention than the president?

Nowhere in the gospel is it written that Jesus ever attempted to meet with Pontius Pilate or King Herod. They were interested in him and received reports from their spies on Jesus's activities. But the King of Kings did not go to the powerful to find favor or impress his friends. No, this king understood where he needed to be. He chose to be with the suffering and the afflicted. He chose to be where he was needed most.

We are often called to be where others will not go, to deal with people no one else wants to handle. We spend more time with the afflicted than with model citizens.

It does not take long to realize that the world is a strange place, with a lot of strange people. From child abuse to cold-blooded murder, we take in a daily diet of serious incidents that often cause us to reassess our lives. You may find yourself asking if there is any hope for those who choose to destroy the innocent. Mark's gospel points out that Jesus came to heal the sick—both the physically sick and spiritually sick—who choose to continue to live in sin and threaten the safety of our streets. The people who are righteous need to continue to live righteously, but those who are spiritually sick need the Great Physician. It is our responsibility to deal with both.

Following Luke 6:37 may seem an impossible task: "Do not judge, and you will not be judged. Do not condemn, and you will not be condemned. Forgive, and you will be forgiven." For example, when we witness a young child who has been living with physical and sexual abuse, it is difficult not to judge the suspect automatically. How can we help but feel this way? If we depend on our own strength, we will judge every time. It is only when we lean on God that we can truly escape our default setting. As police officers, we will witness a great deal of pain and sorrow. Only with God's help will we be able to separate our personal feelings from God's instruction. Remember, we are a resource for public safety, not the judge of people's choices. Our job is to ensure that the innocent and less fortunate are protected.

"The righteous care about justice for the poor, but the wicked have no such concern" (Prov. 29:7). As law enforcement officers, we should be very concerned about the social issues that encourage crime. The overall aspect of public safety is closely tied to community conditions, such as employment, housing, and economic development. We should be concerned about poverty and substandard living conditions. We should identify the poor and the oppressed and work to ease the plight of poverty.

Remember the words of Proverbs 22:2: "Rich and poor have this in common: The Lord is the Maker of them all." While we live in a material world, it is comforting to know that, rich or poor, God looks at everyone the same. The richest man in the community cannot take a shortcut into the Kingdom of God. Riches will not get you ahead; only righteousness will. God is the Creator of us all, and financial wealth does not change that.

Do we react the same way as God? Do we see the poor and the rich alike, or do we set a different standard? If we differentiate, we are negligent in our duties. The poor are often seen as less desirable, but as our lesson on the Beatitudes pointed out, that is not the way God sees the poor—and we shouldn't either. We need to be consistent in everything we do.

We must work to ensure that the less fortunate are given equal rights and service. Often, in poorer communities, the police and other city agencies are all the poor have. They cannot afford doctors, expensive drug counseling, or private education. All they have is what is provided to them through public services. If these services are substandard, then all they will ever receive is substandard care. If you do not ensure justice for them, no one else will. That is the cold reality. We may be the only service they ever receive.

Many communities are wracked by drugs and poverty, two factors that create a vicious cycle. Often, law enforcement agencies spend thousands of hours in these communities only to feel they have accomplished nothing. But this is not true. We may not see all the changes, but they are there. Ask the elderly and the young how they feel about us. Many of them are glad to see us. We give them protection and comfort. Talk to the residents who are not causing problems. They will tell you that they are happy to see us. Don't focus on the negative. Instead, look for the positives and for the people who are happy that we do our job. They are there. Look for them.

In Psalm 12:1 it is written, "Help, Lord for the godly are no more; the faithful have vanished from among men." Though written ages ago, this plea is timely for today. The justice system in America was founded by godly men and established on sound principles and doctrine. It is not the system that is missing the mark; it is the people who operate within it that have fallen short. Though no earthly system will exist without flaw, we should do what is honorable in the eyes of the Creator. Working with the poor and helping ease their burdens is one way to do that.

The world is in constant turmoil. Nowhere is that seen more clearly than in the family unit. Domestic violence is part of every law enforcement officer's job. We see it every day. What some do to their family, we would not do to an animal. The family has become, for some, not a safe haven but a battle zone.

The home is a place of oppression and terror. Wally and Beaver Cleaver do not live there. Instead, we see a world of Jason Voorhees and Freddie Krueger, where people are beaten and humiliated. After seeing how some families function today, we can understand why Plato believed that the family should be eliminated in Utopian society. But that is not what God wants.

Scripture is full of positive admonitions about family. We are told to honor our father and mother and to raise our children on the right path. Even in Jesus's first miracle, we see how important his mother was. At her request, he turned water into wine. He told her it was not his time yet; however, he honored his mother's request.

In today's world, the family can be a disaster, so we should understand our roles as officers. Even when a crime occurs in a family, it is still a crime. It should be handled that way. Family members should be protected, even if only from other family members. For a number of years, many law enforcement agencies acted like crimes within a family were not their business. This was wrong. It is not only our business but our vocation.

This same belief about family should affect our views of the entire community. We should take the time to recognize the underlying problems that affect our job. Our world needs to expand beyond what our eyes see. We should try to see the world as Jesus saw it, with compassion and understanding.

Paul wrote, "Love does no harm to its neighbor. Therefore, love is the fulfillment of the law" (Rom. 13:10). Many times, in the midst of community turmoil and strife, we need to remember to love and care for our community. Hate and anger have no place in a world starving for true love and justice. But God himself is only one source for that love. Romans 13 points out that love is the fulfillment of the law. Without God's love, there is no correction or need to bring a troubled society back to the standard. The standard is God's law. The grace is God's love.

We must renew our souls as often as possible. We should look to Scripture for the answers we seek. God's Word is our ultimate guide. David wrote, "I wait for the Lord, my soul waits, and in His Word I put my hope" (Ps. 130:5). We often ponder what it will take to improve our society. At times, we hope elected officials will rise up to bring the guidance this country needs. Too often, they let us down. When all is said and done, we need to continue to turn to our faith in God. An old hymn says it best, "My hope is built on nothing less than Jesus's blood and righteousness." We need to take that thought with us into duty.

Doesn't it sometimes feel like we are so stressed out that we are just losing ground? Law enforcement is the type of occupation where it is easy to lose perspective. Faith adds balance to a life and career that has its ups and downs. David felt stress too. He cried, "Teach me your way, O Lord; lead me in a straight path because of my oppressors" (Ps. 27:11). This verse serves as a comfort to all who turn to the Lord for instruction. As police officers, we can believe that we actually possess a power to control our destiny, but David understood where his true wisdom came from.

David was the greatest king of Israel and a true warrior. He defeated Goliath. Take the time to go over that story in 1 Samuel 17. Remember, David was the youngest son of Jesse, and King Saul was fighting the Philistines.

For forty days, Goliath mocked Israel and God and made threats against any Israelite who would challenge him: "If he be able to fight with me, and to kill me, then will we be your servants: but if I prevail against him, and kill him, then shall ye be our servants, and serve us" (17:9).

Saul was scared. He had lost faith in his warriors. He had even less faith in David. But David understood where his power came from. He said, "The Lord that delivered me out of the paw of the lion, and out of the paw of the bear, he will deliver me out of the hand of this Philistine" (17:37). David refused to wear the armor Saul gave him. He chose instead to face Goliath with five smooth stones, his sling, and his faith in God. Goliath thought it was some kind of joke when he saw David. Goliath asked, "Am I a dog?" (17:43). He did not take David seriously.

We all know what happened next. David killed the giant and went on to greatness. But David was also a flawed man who would experience many trials and tribulations. When he was down and out, he went to the Father.

If society is in need, then its servants also need assistance. In law enforcement, the "macho factor" for men and women can get out of control. We feel we shouldn't need help and believe we are above assistance. However, if King David needed renewal in a broken world, so do we. If the greatest warrior can humbly bow before God, we should be able to do that too.

Scripture continuously reminds us that God can help us in a world in need. Let's consider a few key verses together.

"The Lord is close to the brokenhearted and saves those who are crushed in spirit" (Ps. 34:18).

Relationships are difficult for everyone. A failing relationship has been the downfall of a number of good men and women, including police officers. We all care for others, and when that happens, we stand a chance of entering the zone of the brokenhearted. Relationships can be difficult. It takes the work of two people to make a partnership successful. A partner also has to have a forgiving and understanding heart. We are not saying, "Do not love or trust." Rather, we ask you to remember that relationships involve two people who, at times, will make mistakes. Can you forgive? God does.

"The righteous man may have many troubles, but the Lord delivers him from them all" (Ps. 34:19).

As police officers, we find ourselves surrounded by darkness. In our daily dealings with people who represent evil, it is comforting to know that the Lord will deliver us from the power of darkness.

"Consider the blameless, observe the upright; there is a future for the man of peace" (Ps. 37:37).

Teen violence is a troubling trend in America today. Our youth are in critical need of consistent models in the area of conflict and violence prevention. As a country, we turn to violence too quickly. In many cases, we abandon problem-solving efforts, and with a lack of self-control, we turn to violent means. But throughout his life, Jesus was a peacemaker. Time after time, he set an example of bringing peace to a world full of hate. Our God is a God of peace. There is a future for the man of peace, so we should make it a priority to display God's peace to the world.

"How good and pleasant it is when brothers live together in unity" (Ps. 133:1).

Racial tension and strife are a constant thorn in our side as a society. Too many individuals have hearts and minds full of hate for those of a different race or culture. In law enforcement, we recognize that race is a factor in many hate crimes. To accept one another is a basic Christian principle. We must love each other, regardless of race, creed, color, and sex. Now, that is good cultural diversity training.

"But it is God who judges: He brings one down, he exalts another" (Ps. 75:7).

The greatest peace in life comes from believing that God is in control. While we struggle to be recognized by those around us, it is God who will be the judge of our ways. Even though it is nice to get along with other people, true peace and freedom comes from knowing what other people think of us is not important. Experience real freedom by working to please God and by seeking our King. Isaiah wrote, "Seek the Lord while he may be found; call on him while he is near" (Is. 55:6).

"A man can do nothing better than to eat and drink and find satisfaction in his work" (Eccles. 2:24).

Have you ever experienced the torment of working around people who are not satisfied with their job? In law enforcement, we face problems that lend themselves to job dissatisfaction. Some police officers are not happy about anything. While part of this problem is human nature, the real issue is that public servants who are not happy with their jobs make it hard on those they come into contact with. Working in public service can be a struggle, but to be successful, we must enjoy what we do. Do yourself a favor: if you are not happy with your work, change it.

"All a man's ways seem innocent to him, but motives are weighed by the Lord" (Prov. 16:2).

As law enforcement officers, we are consistently asked to prove others' motives. In some cases, this is difficult. It is hard to know someone's motives without examining his heart. As people struggle to prove themselves righteous in the eyes of their fellow man, we can be assured that God will hold the scale. While God is in control, he needs dedicated law enforcement officers to search out the evil motives of a sinful society.

"Carry each other's burdens and in this way you will fulfill the law of Christ" (Gal. 6:2).

Police officers have always been recognized as a brotherhood. One bonding factor is the reality that the world is viewed differently by those who are called to police it. We are also joined together in bearing the unique burden of our positions. At times, law enforcement responsibilities can weigh us down. Look around for a friend to help carry a share of your weight.

God's words are as important today as at any other time. We face a world in crisis and a society in need. Often, we are facing our own demons while trying to help others. It is a daunting task, but we can handle it. Like David, we can trust God to give us strength to get the job done. Like Jesus and his disciples, we can go where others fear to tread. We can reach for the higher calling, knowing that Jesus has asked this of us.

We can be victorious. We can help those less fortunate. We can make a difference.

CHAPTER REFLECTIONS

- It is not the healthy who need a doctor but the sick.
- Do not judge, and you will not be judged.
- A righteous spirit will become the light for a society in darkness.
- True public safety is the right of the poor as well as the rich.
- We are all rich in God's eyes; we are his creation.
- True godliness starts with the true Creator.
- Love and law are God's plan. All other ground is sinking sand.
- The Lord is my teacher.
- The Lord is close to a broken heart.
- Don't just tell them Jesus loves them; tell them you're willing to love them too.
- Role models needed. Serious men and women apply.
- Faith is being certain of what we do not see.
- It is God who judges.
- Call on the Lord while he is near.
- God calls us to like what we do.
- Our motives are weighed by God.
- Carry each other, and the Lord will carry you both.

PRAYER FOR A SOCIETY IN NEED

Lord God, place your life-changing power on the spiritually sick and open their eyes to a life free from the chains of sin. Grant me the strength to put away my personal feelings when it comes to judging others. Use me to show them the way, not to condemn them. Give me hope in a world of darkness. Thank you for your promise to deliver me from the troubles I face as I live righteously for you. Bless the poor and open our eyes to help those in our community who are oppressed.

Thank you for your acceptance of all people. Thank you that, rich or poor, you love us all the same. Lead us in a renewal of the ideals that founded the very system we uphold in your name. Thank you for showing me how love fulfills what you intended. Direct me to that love. Teach me your way. Fill me with your wisdom. Help mend our broken hearts. Teach me to lean on your strength. Amen.

CHAPTER 5
THE EYES OF A CHILD

Imagine how our society must look through the eyes of a child or young adult. The world is full of greed and hate, with people fighting throughout America. Fortunately, Jesus has a special place for children and, as law enforcement officers, so should we. In Matthew 19:14, Jesus said, "Let the little children come to me, and do not hinder them, for the kingdom of heaven belongs to such as these." These strong words should be taken to heart. Jesus was an advocate for the weak and helpless. Many children in today's society fit that description. They are at the mercy of the world.

In today's law enforcement environment, we are able to make a great impact on young people. We can serve as mentors, educators, and role models. Today's young people, more than ever, are looking for role models. After the destruction of September 11th, many took notice of the heroic work of firefighters and law enforcement officers. They were amazed that men and women were willing to risk—and even sacrifice—their lives for strangers. People who work in these professions know that we have been doing that for years. Often underappreciated and underpaid, we are still willing to do the job. And we do it out of a sense of duty and commitment. These are the types of role models that young people and all of society need. We should be ready to take that role and lead the young people in our communities.

Law enforcement has expanded beyond traditional roles. No longer are we just detectives and beat officers; we are educators and teachers. Through drug and bullying education programs, we go into classrooms and discuss the problems that exist in our culture. We hope to proactively educate young people and their parents.

We strive to educate young people *before* they get involved with drugs. We have a responsibility to share the truth with them because we have seen the destruction and death drugs bring. We need to share the less glamorous side of the drug trade, but we are up against movies and music that make drugs appear harmless. We know better, and it's our responsibility to share that information.

Police agencies often look down on these roles. Officers involved in these education initiatives are called "kiddy cops" or "the rubber gun squad." It is a shame that this attitude prevails because the problems we face in the schools are just as tough as what is happening on the streets. It should be the goal of everyone in law enforcement to practice prevention. Community safety has a vital role in society.

Reaching young people before they go astray can save dollars, heartache, and lives. This is the way youth crime prevention should be viewed, and this view is backed by scripture: "How can a young man keep his way pure? By living according to your word" (Ps. 119:9). Many want a quick fix to juvenile crime in America as this problem is costing our communities a tremendous amount in tax revenue. A number of current programs are solid efforts to save our youth, but the real answers come from the Word. Young people need education to make good choices along the way, and the Bible is a great place to start. As law officers, we should model what it preaches.

Unfortunately, it is impossible in most public-school settings to give the message of Christ. However, we can model the behavior and show compassion and understanding. We can share our experiences about life.

"Train a child in the way he should go, and when he is old, he will not turn from it" (Prov. 22:6).

Children are a special gift from God for us to treasure and cherish. Having children is more than an event. It is a lifetime of responsibility. Today, we see parents who have neglected the task of raising their children; these young people become statistics in our juvenile justice system. Teaching children is a full-time endeavor that is never complete. However, some parents are not able or willing to handle this task. They expect everyone else to pick up their slack.

This might not seem fair, but it is the truth. It is not enough to say it is not our job and walk away because, in law enforcement, we may see these individuals again. When we see these people again, however, they may have guns. The world has changed as it's become more violent. We are called to address that issue.

Since the shooting at Columbine High School, a greater emphasis has been placed on school safety. The school resource officer (SRO) at Columbine and the officers who arrived on the scene later did not feel they were "kiddy cops" or "the rubber gun squad." They understood immediately the crisis at hand. Most of us would never want to be in that situation; we should pray for the officers who were. Schools are a microcosm of society. We should be there to handle the problems before they become a full-blown crisis.

SROs provide security to schools and surrounding neighborhoods. They are responsible for providing routine patrols and making contact with citizens living around the school. SROs have an opportunity to work closely with parents who are experiencing problems with their children.

On one such occasion, parents and administrators were concerned about problems from the neighborhood affecting their local school. Several teenage females had been in numerous physical altercations, and rumors were circulating that these girls were going to fight at the school. The school's SRO, in conjunction with the Youth Services Division, arranged a meeting with the students, their parents, and school administrators. The situation was resolved without further incident.

Officers who work these assignments say that each school is like its own city. They feel they are better able to handle the problems that arise since they are allowed to focus their entire attention on the school and are able to build a relationship with the students. The students learn to trust the SRO, who can then work with students before a problem escalates. Administrators, police officers, and school staff talk about the positive impact the SRO program has had on students.

SROs are not just there for enforcement. They are responsible for crime prevention and serve as role models. They are not only police officers but also educators. The SRO is a valuable part of the school team, and their knowledge of the law is invaluable to the school staff. The

SRO is in a unique position, not only to enforce the law but to also explain its purpose and its importance.

Schools and the communities they serve cannot be separated. If problems plague the neighborhood, they will impact the school, and school-based problems will eventually filter into the neighborhood they serve. Therefore, schools and the community must unite and accept the responsibility of school safety. No police partnership is greater than the one we have with schools.

The reputation of an entire city can be influenced by people's perception of crime and education in that area. An active partnership between schools and police can greatly impact public perception and overall view of the community.

When we understand this concept, we understand why law enforcement must play a role in the relationship between the schools and our society. It is imperative that we share our knowledge with the youth of today. We should be in schools to educate and guide.

It is a great challenge to accomplish all the things we have listed in this chapter, but it is important that we try. Our communities are counting on us, and we have a responsibility to the young people in our schools.

And let's not forget our own young ones. As parents, God expects a great deal from us. He wouldn't have us give our children to the community to rear. He depends on us to do it. Neglecting our children is like destroying one of God's precious creatures. If you are looking for a good parenting class, you might consider the Bible. The book of Proverbs would be a great place to begin. Remember to train your children in the way of the Lord.

We often get overwhelmed in our profession. We work extra jobs, prepare for court, review law materials, and maintain our equipment. This is all done in addition to our daily workload. In these busy times, don't forget your children. They may not remember if you had the shiniest gear on the shift, but they will remember the baseball game you attended together. They may not have any idea that you were officer of the year, but they will remember if you were a good parent. No one would ask you to neglect your job, but do not neglect your children either.

Your children only have one childhood. No matter how much time you spend with them when they are adults, you can never make up the time you lost from their childhood. Each child has only one first day of kindergarten, one fifth-grade Christmas play, and one sixteenth birthday. Do not miss them. Remember Jesus's words for those who might treat children poorly: "It were better for him that a millstone were hanged about his neck, and he cast into the sea, than that he should offend one of these little ones" (Luke 17:2). Believe that he meant it. Our children are important, and Christ takes our responsibility as parents seriously.

CHAPTER REFLECTIONS

- The kingdom of heaven belongs to children and such as these.
- It is every adult's responsibility to ensure safety for the young.
- A young man keeps his way pure by living according to the Word.
- Model the Word of the Lord, and others will see the Savior.
- Train a child in the way he should go, and when he is old, he will not turn from it.
- A child will do what he sees as much as what he is told.
- Never cause a young one to stumble.
- Be there to show the road to righteousness.
- Jesus has a special place for the weak and needy.
- Minister to those who need assistance.
- Raise your children with the Word of the Lord.
- Never neglect your own.

PRAYER FOR THE EYES OF A CHILD

Lord, allow me to see through the eyes of a child. Let me understand that the weak should be protected. Give me an opportunity to reach those you call me to protect. Give me the patience to stay on the right course.

Allow me to be a role model. Give me the strength to tell the truth in all situations. Never let me forget my own children. They are your gift to me. Keep them in your blessing and keep them in my heart in all matters. Give me the wisdom to make them job number one. Amen.

CHAPTER 6
DEFINING LOVE

ove is a strange word to use in any book about law enforcement. You'll find no love section in the police academy manual. Paul, however, felt strongly about love. In twenty-first century America, when we think of love, it's romantic love or maybe the love we feel for a family member. The word *love* has an intimate quality to it. It is a word we use to describe our feelings toward those we care about most. We may say we love football, TV, or reading books, but when it comes to people, we only use this word for those who are special.

Sometimes saying, "I love you," can be difficult. The same people who say they love their dog may have trouble saying they love their best friend or relatives. They may even have trouble saying it about their immediate family.

Others suffer emotionally because those closest to them could not say, "I love you." It is a shame. Love is a natural emotion.

Jesus said, "Love your enemy." He did not mean find the person you dislike the most and take him or her on a date. He was talking about respect, about treating others the way we would like to be treated. He was talking about empathy as much as emotion. In the King James Version the word for *love* is translated *charity*. In this translation, it may be easier to understand that *love* is not a romantic love.

Time and time again, Jesus makes reference to the way we treat each other. And time and time again, he shows our shortcomings. Jesus pointed out how quick we are to expose other people's problems while ignoring our own. We all have done that without even realizing it.

When Jesus chastised the scribes and Pharisees, he talked about how they used the law to burden people, not to bring them closer to God. Jesus wants to liberate people, not cage them. He talked about doing these things for the Kingdom of God. We should follow his lead.

Do not confuse love with a romantic feeling. Do not confuse it with the feelings you have for your family. It's about compassion and respect. It's about showing people today what the Kingdom of God will look like when the Son of Man returns.

We, as Christians, are called to complete this task. It is part of our everyday mission, and it is a tough task. Without the power of Jesus, it cannot be accomplished.

Paul wrote the most powerful verses regarding love. They are simple, but their depth should not be missed. They call us to reach above the limits of our humanity. And the toughest part is that we are called to love not only those we care for but also our enemies. In Matthew 5: 46-48, we read Jesus's words: "For if ye love them which love you, what reward have ye? Do not even the publicans the same? And if ye salute your brethren only, what do ye more than theirs? Do not even the publicans so? Be ye therefore perfect, even as your Father which is in heaven is perfect." For many of us, that may be the most difficult assignment we are given in law enforcement. But, if Jesus did not think we could accomplish it with his help, he would not have given us the assignment.

Let's take time to review what Paul said about love and how it applies to our day-to-day lives, both at work and at home. Paul's ideas about life may seem simple, but they are also complex. We should strive every day to accomplish our mission of walking in the footsteps of the Lord.

"Love is patient, love is kind. It does not envy, it does not boast, it is not proud" (1 Cor. 13:4).

Some of the most complicated situations we handle in law enforcement are domestic. When we are called to homes where people cannot get along peacefully, it becomes easy to believe that no one understands love in the first place. First Corinthians 13 outlines the different qualities connected to the word *love*, but let us also consider all that love is not. We learn that love is patient and kind, but we also read that love is *not* found in envy, boasting, or pride. How many times have you seen a person's pride get them in trouble?

During domestics, even after police arrive, the individuals arguing still want to make their point. Even after they have been arrested, they are not humble. They are still trying to prove their side of the argument. Often, it is not until they are alone in a cell that they realize how much trouble they are in. Immersed in argument, the individuals failed to realize how out of control the situation had become.

In our own lives, do we allow this principle to rule? Are we unkind? Do we envy? Are we boastful? We shouldn't be. Instead, we should seize every opportunity to be kind and humble. This becomes particularly imperative when dealing with victims. They have already been victimized once by the perpetrator. They should not be victimized again by our lack of compassion or smug attitude.

"Love is not rude, it is not self-seeking, it is not easily angered, it keeps no record of wrongs" (1 Cor. 13:5).

How many times have you witnessed one or both participants in a domestic situation being rude to one another? One of the biggest problems facing relationships in America is the lack of self-control concerning rudeness and anger. It is amazing to see how many profess love for someone whom they treat badly. The Bible teaches us that love is not rude or quick to anger. If a person really loves someone, he or she should treat that person in a special way. Remember to focus on love as Paul outlines, not as the world knows it. Real love compels us to hold deep respect for others.

Rudeness can bring devastation, making others feel insignificant, not worthy of common decency. Treat people the way you want to be treated. If someone treats us with disrespect, we want to strike out against them angrily. If you are rude to people, they likewise feel they have been cheated of respect and, therefore, do not owe you any respect. It creates an awful cycle that, if not controlled, can lead to violence. Rudeness is never correct.

Love is not self-seeking. It focuses on the other and puts the other first. Love does not get mad or hold grudges. Rather, it looks for opportunities to serve.

Have you ever observed an officer who thought he was being wronged every time he went on a call? It was awful that he had to take a report or deal with people. It was awful that the person didn't avoid the crime that had inconvenienced him. If you listened to this officer long enough, you would think he was victimized. Even before the case went to court, he would complain about the justice system. Everything was about him. This is a serious situation because the person was no longer focused on his responsibilities. And when those are forgotten, problems are sure to follow.

"Love does not delight in evil but rejoices in the truth" (1 Cor. 13:6).

The best way to build a successful relationship is through honesty. The couple who believes in being truthful and open with one another stands an excellent chance of having a great relationship. Paul expresses the importance of truth in defining love. Successful marriages are built on honesty. We all long for a bond with our spouse that is safe enough to open our minds and hearts to each other. Rejoicing in the truth is a definite cause for celebration in today's world. But always remember that the truth may be uncomfortable at times. When we face a point where the truth hurts, our honesty may be tested. This also is where relationships are tested. But keep in mind that the truth will bring freedom to your relationships.

In our workplace, truth is all we have. Once we have compromised the truth, we can no longer do our job effectively. There is no reason for officers to lie, even if they feel the person does not deserve their rights. Lies are the enemy of police work. It is the destroyer that ruins police departments. Honesty is all you have. Do not compromise yourself.

> *"Love always protects, always trusts, always hopes, always perseveres"* (1 Cor. 13:7).

When we think of what makes a successful relationship, we should consider the word *trust*. A relationship not centered on trust will eventually fail. As police officers, the ability to trust does not come easily. We continue to spend a great deal of time with individuals who make it difficult to trust. This is a critical area of our lives that, if we are not careful, could cause problems in our personal relationships. To understand love is to give up any hesitation to trust. Remember to stay in touch with the ability to trust.

Trust is also an important element of your job. Without trust, it is impossible to do our jobs. We have to depend on each other. We have to know that, through thick and thin, we can count on our peers. If an officer shows he cannot be trusted, it destroys the morale of his entire shift.

Law enforcement agencies should also work to build trust in the community. We should be working with other agencies to show that we are committed to our citizens. We should be meeting people face to face and sharing our goals and concerns. We should make citizens part of the solution to neighborhood problems.

Be open with your community. Share information with civic organizations so they understand the tasks we have throughout our cities and towns. If citizens feel they have an open police department, they will feel it can be trusted. If they sense the department is secretive, they will feel the organization has something to hide.

"And now these three remain: faith, hope and love. But the greatest of these is love" (1 Cor. 13:13).

In the thirteenth chapter of 1 Corinthians, Paul cleared up any questions about the importance of love. It has been said, "They will know we are Christians by our love" (John 13:35). One of the greatest problems we face in modern-day society is that, at times, Christians have not exhibited love. We must keep in mind that it is easy to display love as the world knows it, but our challenge is to show others *God's love*. Remember, as you encounter worldly ideas and issues, don't rely on *Webster's Dictionary* for the definition of love. Go to God's Word.

God's love is peace, and it is always unconditional for all who come to him.

Love is not a word often associated with police work, but it should be. We're not speaking of the romantic love you see in the movies but of real love. Giving love is giving respect. Giving love is showing compassion. Giving love is doing our job with mercy.

CHAPTER REFLECTIONS

- Love is patient; love is kind.
- Love is not rude.
- Love is truth in action.
- Love equals trust.
- Love your enemies.
- Even sinners love those who love them.
- Show the love of the Father.
- Show people today the Kingdom of God.
- The greatest gift is love.

PRAYER FOR LOVE

Lord, teach us the true meaning of love and help us truly to love one another. Continue to show us the path of love. Help our relationships to be built on truth. Give us the ability to trust. Help us to stay in touch with our trusting ability. Thank you for giving us a true definition of love and help us to live by it.

Allow us to love our enemies. Allow us to be an example for all to see. Show the Kingdom of God to come through my actions. Amen.

CHAPTER 7
GOD'S WAY

Often, we ask ourselves which way we should go. With so many ideas circulating in society, it is easy to get confused or look to others for solutions. However, we should keep our eyes on the prize and stay committed to the ways of our Lord. In the early Christian Church, the gospel was referred to as "the Way."

Let's reflect on some Bible verses that can help us focus on what God has to say about our world. For the Word is as relevant today as it was when it was written.

God is concerned about your day-to-day life. Jesus said, "Do not worry about tomorrow, for tomorrow will worry about itself. Each day has enough trouble of its own" (Matt. 6:34). Live every day to the fullest. In our profession, we witness the tragedy of a life suddenly taken.

This hopefully makes us realize that life is a gift and each day should be treasured. Under the weight of our work, we may fail to appreciate the little things in life. Because of all we see, it is easy to lose the joy that life has to offer and instead live a life of worry. Do you ever wonder what tomorrow may bring, what issues or problems will you face? Jesus encourages us not to worry about tomorrow, and we should live out that advice. After all, it comes from someone who knows a lot about control.

It can be difficult to avoid the trap of worry. In fact, worry can even make us forget our own salvation as we become consumed by the darkness of the material world. John wrote about that darkness and man's desire to stay in the darkness: "This is the verdict: Light has come into the world, but men loved darkness instead of light, because their deeds were evil" (John 3:19). The plan of salvation that leads us to eternal life is clearly laid out in John's gospel. But even today, many continue to reject the plan. By turning away from God's truth, we also move away from the promise of eternal life. In this verse from John, it is interesting to note that men loved darkness so they rejected the light, Jesus Christ. It is disheartening to know that, even today, many still love darkness. For this reason, we witness a great deal of that darkness as law enforcement officers. While society searches for answers to the problems of this world, Jesus still stands at the door and knocks. Do we always answer?

When we replace our relationship with Jesus with the worries of the world, we run the risk of forgetting who is in control. During these times, we need to focus on our personal relationship with the Son of Man. Jesus declared, "I am the bread of life. He who comes to me will never go hungry, and he who believes in me will never be thirsty" (John 6:35). Many in our business will not confess their level of anxiety. But worry is present in most who choose this job. Job and personal stressors are easier to handle with a strong faith in God. Jesus explains that he is all-sufficient to provide even our basic needs. If Jesus has promised to fulfill the basics, we certainly must believe that our greatest concerns and fears will be handled by the Great Physician.

It is imperative that we take time each day to worship and reflect on our relationship with Christ. Communication is an essential part of our lives here on earth. Most important is our communication with our commander-in-chief, the Lord God Almighty. Prayer helps us through some tough moments as police officers. Communication with God always brings a form of peace to our mind and soul. Some people are afraid of prayer, and I believe it is because they don't know how to pray. The greatest lesson on prayer comes from the master himself in Matthew 6:9-13:

This is how you should pray:
Our father in heaven, hallowed be your name
Your kingdom come, your will be done
on earth as it is in heaven.
Forgive us our debts, as we also have forgiven our
debtors.
And lead us not into temptation,
but deliver us from the evil one.

Prayer is important. We should take time each day to fellowship with Christ. It is during these times that we build our faith and grow spiritually. Unfortunately, the word *faith* has become a widely used term to describe almost every type of relationship known to man. At times, we may be guilty of taking faith too lightly. Hebrews 11:1 gives us the true definition of *faith*: "Faith is being sure of what we hope for and certain of what we do not see." While it is good to have faith in each other, we need to remember that the central energy of our faith must be directed toward God. While the world encourages us to place our faith in the things of this world, we keep in mind that all of our earthly possessions will fade away. As sad as it may seem, even our treasured earthly relationships will someday fade away. The only relationship we know will never end is the one we share with the Creator.

As Christians, "We live by faith, but not by sight" (2 Cor. 5:7). At times, faith is an extremely difficult concept to understand. The human side of faith would tell us that you should believe in that which you can see, hear, and touch. It is easy to get distracted by the physical world. But what about air? You really can't see it or touch it, but you know it is there. You have faith that we'll have plenty of air to breathe. God is like that. You can't physically see God or touch him, but spiritually, you can experience him and much more if you only believe. When we experience him, we know it. This example should renew your faith and help you understand it. Understand that we have been given the blessing of knowing there is more to this world than just what we can see, hear, and touch.

Since we have this knowledge, our faith and trust should be placed in the Lord. He is the provider of all our needs. Scripture says, "It is better to take refuge in the Lord than to trust man" (Ps. 118:8). An important lesson to learn is to be extra careful in where you place your trust, as far as people are concerned. Through the years, many held in high esteem have fallen because of the trust factor. Because of what we observe in our job in law enforcement, it can be difficult to trust. Psalm 118:8 should encourage us to place our trust in the Lord and not in man. The nature of man is to sin and fall short. But God is always there. God's power is something to trust. Our trust and faith in the Lord give us spiritual growth.

In our duties as police officers, we see conflict and the struggle between good and evil. We see those who embrace the light and those who choose to live in darkness. Even as we deal with our peers, we see the same struggles. Unfortunately, not everyone observes the world through Christian eyes. Christian officers have often complained that their views are not accepted on their watch or shift. They feel as if they are being told that the Christian perspective is not strong enough. Christian officers have to fight this misconception. Jesus gives us the tools we need to serve the world. His disciplines are necessary to become a successful police officer. We should never move away from the principles of God.

Peter wrote, "However, if you suffer as a Christian, do not be ashamed, but praise God that you bear that name" (1 Pet. 4:16). It has been said throughout the ages that politics and religion do not mix. Many people take this to the extreme by challenging the right of public employees to express their faith in connection with their jobs. Resist the idea that we are wrong for expressing our faith when others challenge it. Those around us may criticize our beliefs, but we must be counted for the cause of Christ. We must stand up for what we believe in, not only by our words but by our actions as well.

It is not enough to say you are a Christian. We have to live out our faith, even when it is difficult. We belong completely to Christ. Our actions should show that commitment. Others will be watching after they discover you are a believer. They want to see how you act. Some will observe you because they want to learn how to follow Christ. Others will watch to see if you stumble. It's a giant responsibility, but we have a giant God to help us.

The Apostle Paul had a lot in common with today's law enforcement officers. He spent the majority of his life trying to get people to follow the straight and narrow road. Many he was called to serve had openly violated God's law. Paul had to suffer due to his calling to serve others, but he continued to hold on to one basic truth. He fully believed that all of his suffering would never compare to the glory God has in store for his followers. Today's law enforcement officer faces a great deal of ridicule and pressure from a shattered society. As public servants, we must learn to follow Paul's example by focusing on the prize and not the race. Paul wrote, "I consider that our present sufferings are not worth comparing with the glory that will be revealed in us" (Rom. 8:18). In times of crisis, these words should keep us strong.

The road to heaven is difficult. Jesus knew many would hear his words, but few would follow. He told his followers of the dilemma: "But small is the gate and narrow the road that leads to life, and only a few find it" (Matt. 7:14). The United States Marines are famous for the popular slogan, "We are looking for a few good men." The Marines are seeking those who would be interested in a challenge. In the book of Matthew, Jesus issues a similar challenge. Being a follower on the way to the kingdom is not easy.

Jesus points out that the path to the kingdom is narrow and only a few will find it.

Jesus understood that the task is difficult and that we would have to stay committed to him to accomplish our goals. He gave us grace and understanding to help us with our journey.

We need to remember our gifts as we tackle our responsibilities. Our goals at work should always focus on our relationship with Christ. Even our worldly ambitions should focus on the Lord. Paul wrote, "Make it your ambition to lead a quiet life, to mind your own business and to work with your hands, just as we told you" (1 Thess. 4:11). Have you thought about your life's ambition? Normally when we think of ambition, we have grand visions of making a great deal of money or finding fame. We envision what the world considers an ambitious person. Ambition should be what you possess inside to lead you to success as you see it. We need to remember that ambition, to some, may be simple things we can accomplish. Scripture challenges us to make it our ambition to lead a quiet life and to mind our own business. When we think of the problems facing today's society, this could be a great example for a number of people.

The Bible encourages believers not to seek an earthly reward. Jesus clearly believes that worldly gain has nothing to do with eternal reward. Jesus was committed to the Kingdom of God, not the kingdom of man. He saw everyone as equal in the eyes of God. Proverbs 22:2 states, "Rich and poor have this in common: The Lord is the Maker of them all." It is hard to imagine that the rich and poor in our society would have anything in common. To be rich in this world is to have a life centered around material wealth. The truth is that lasting wealth has nothing to do with what you own. Money is a tool for trade, but the Lord has created each of us with special worth. A person's wealth is not on his bank statement but within his heart and soul. The Lord is the maker of all people, and they are all wealthy in the eyes of the Creator.

In Jesus's conversation with the rich ruler, it becomes obvious that money can even hinder a person's relationship with God. The quest for material reward can outweigh the need for personal salvation. Money should not be our primary goal.

We should strive to be satisfied with what we have. The quest for more money and more things can be disastrous. Proverbs offers wisdom on this situation: "The rich rule over the poor, and the borrower is servant to the lender" (Prov. 22:7). While the pay for law enforcement officers has greatly improved, it still falls short of the wages common in corporate America. Most would say you should not choose to be in public safety for the money. However, debt is a tremendous problem for many decent families. The cost of living in our country has insured a certain amount of debt for most Americans. The key to financial success is in Scripture: maintain a position with your debts that allows you to be the controller of your financial destiny. Proverbs presents the idea that the borrower is a servant to the lender. Are you a servant to your debtors?

Money should not be our only goal as police officers. We should be focused on the task at hand. We should be committed to giving our communities the service they deserve. Proverbs 10:16 says, "The wages of the righteous bring them life, but the income of the wicked brings them punishment." An honest day's work still matters in a time when many try to take shortcuts in their work ethic. It is refreshing to meet those who still believe in giving their best effort. The book of Proverbs is a blueprint for the honest workers of America. Proverbs 10:16 promises that the righteous will earn more than money in their lifetime. But, more important, Scripture points out that the income of the wicked will bring them punishment. Those who believe that they will not face the consequences for gaining wealth through dishonest means need to take a good look. More than one police officer has lost focus and lost everything they own.

We owe employers a good day's work for our wages. America is experiencing a breakdown in its long-standing work ethic. Many citizens will not work. The Bible is clear on the issue of hard work. Jesus surrounded himself with people who were workers. A good example would be the disciples who followed Jesus on a non-stop schedule in tough conditions. It would be hard to find a time when these men gave up or when one of them refused to work. Proverbs 19:15 states, "Laziness brings on deep sleep, and the shiftless man goes hungry." So, for those who sit and wait on the world to give them their reward, it is time to get up and roll up your sleeves.

Often those who do the least amount of work on a shift are also the biggest malcontents. Through their words and actions, they destroy a watch or shift. We should make sure we avoid this trap by not aligning ourselves with people who are negative and by not allowing others to dictate the type of day we are having. It is our responsibility to maintain control of our attitude. God has produced a great world full of nature and beauty, but we are quick to ignore that fact and move on to issues that won't matter in the end. Make a commitment to stay positive and committed to your job. Being negative has never accomplished anything.

We should be on guard to ensure that everything we do is not based on earthly rewards. The Bible teaches us that we should treasure our reward that is yet to come, the day we shall share in the kingdom of heaven. Psalm 17:14 states, "O Lord, by your hand save me from such men, from men of this world whose reward is in this life." To-day's world believes every good deed must be rewarded. As a Christian, our reward is not of this world. We should perform good deeds because God has called us to a righteous task. While others seek out earthly rewards, let us focus on the rewards yet to come in glory, the rewards that matter.

During our lives, we should be committed to showing the glory of God in all of our actions. People should be able to tell we are Christians by our words and deeds: "May the words of my mouth and the meditation of my heart be pleasing in your sight, O Lord, my Rock and my Redeemer" (Ps. 19:14). As law enforcement officers, we hear some of the crudest comments from people in society. At times, these comments are made by police officers. We need to be careful of our words. Our speech should be honorable to those around us and at all times pleasing to God. People are easily judged by their oral communication, and as law enforcement officers, we are closely monitored for what we say. Keep in mind the six ears present in every conversation we have: ours, the other person's, and God's.

Righteous living can be a tough task, but Jesus has given us the strength to accomplish our goal. Proverbs 4:25 says, "Let your eyes look straight ahead, fix your gaze directly before you."

Today's society presents a number of difficult challenges for us. In law enforcement, as we attempt to solve community problems, it may become easy to lose our focus and priorities. We live in a society where transition and change are evident, but during the change, we still need to remain focused. As Christians, God would have us remain on track with our eyes fixed on the issue at hand. Remember, when we lose our focus, we move away from our goals and objectives.

We live in a world where some people don't just live in darkness, they enjoy living in darkness, for it is where they feel comfortable. They seem to treat the value of life in a lighthearted way. Life is precious, so we should shudder when we meet those who take it for granted. As police officers, we know we should be brave, but it should be frightening to witness those who do not care how they leave the earth. They give no regard to human life.

What is the value of life in America? For many people, it is minimal. How many parents and loved ones have looked over crime scene tapes and seen a loved one lying murdered in the street? How many have seen loved ones being photographed as evidence? It is disheartening to see the unnecessary suffering.

The men and women who live this lifestyle would be surprised to know there are two sets of laws: man's law and God's law. They have rejected God's law, and, therefore, man's laws are irrelevant. To sin is to violate God's law, and the Bible teaches us that sin is lawlessness: "Everyone who sins breaks the law; in fact, sin is lawlessness" (I John 3:4). It is impossible for someone who rejects all ideas of sin to be lawful.

The fool says in his heart, "There is no God" (Ps. 14:1). Life can be full of mistakes and misfortunes, and one of the biggest mistakes a person can make is to say in his heart that there is no God. The Bible labels such person a fool. As law enforcement officers, we constantly get caught up in the routine of a sin-ridden society. We have a front-row seat to the ravages of sin. We have seen the destruction of life and property. We have seen the consequence of lawlessness.

In regard to what is truth, Americans continue to struggle. Truth is not a simple belief or feeling. It is a deep-rooted lifestyle that only comes through a personal relationship with the Savior, who is the Author of Truth. Truth is the cornerstone of integrity. Jesus taught the importance of truth in John 8:32: "You will know the truth, and the truth will set you free." Remember, this is not truth as the world knows it but truth that only comes from God. So, while the world continues to search for what they call truth, let's have our daily spiritual walk with the Founder of Truth.

Our job can be discouraging at times. It is difficult to measure the support of the community when all those we come in contact with are citizens in crisis. In this occupation, we will not make a great deal of money, but we can have a different type of satisfaction for our public service. Hebrews 6:19 has a great deal to say about the service we provide: "God is not unjust, he will not forget your work and the love you have shown him as you have helped his people and continue to help them." Our good deeds are in the thoughts of the Creator. God is not unjust. He will reward those who serve, those who are his faithful.

Stay focused on the Word and be ready to learn and grow in the Lord. Most Christians are eager to learn and take in all the knowledge they can gain. But some would have you believe that they know everything, that you certainly could not tell them anything new. Paul was a great preacher and teacher. He continually provided those he came in contact with a word of truth or instruction. He points out the importance of accepting instruction s life is a learning process. We should go into each day wanting to learn something new and different. Make it a personal goal each day to receive a word of instruction.

We should be on guard that we do not become proud and boastful. We need to remember constantly the price Jesus has paid for each of us. At times it becomes easy to believe that, since we are involved in a career that creates justice, our good works will keep us safe. However, the Bible clearly teaches that our effort has nothing to do with earning eternal life. It is God's mercy, not our works, that allows us to enter the Kingdom of God. So, while we are involved in an honorable occupation, our jobs alone will not win us eternal life. We must accept Christ and live by his commandments. Romans 9:16 clearly states, "It does not, therefore, depend on man's desire or effort, but on God's mercy."

We should not get egotistical about status and how we are perceived. Politics can be involved in almost all aspects of society. In law enforcement, we are constantly around the political arena. It can be disheartening to realize that many community leaders and police officers have forgotten who they work for. Leaders at the local, state, and national level are called to serve, not to be served. While it is important to respect our leaders, realize that they—and we—have an obligation to become servants ourselves. Jesus was clear when he said that the people who are first must also be open to serve others. He stated, "If anyone wants to be first, he must be the very last, and the servant of all" (Mark 9:35). When is the last time you saw a congressman wash someone's feet? When was the last time you did that? Jesus did, and he asks us to do the same.

During our lives, it is easy to forget why we serve. It is easy to forget our commitment to Christ. Have you ever wished you could start over again? Maybe there's a period of time you would like to forget. You might have experienced the aftermath of a poor decision. It could have been a mistake that you made at work or in your personal life. Second Corinthians 5:17 says, "Therefore if any man be in Christ, he is a new creation; old things are passed away, behold all thing are become new." This verse clarifies what life is like with Christ. Every day with the Lord is a new day and a new beginning. What grace and mercy are given to those who are in Christ! Life is exciting because we have a new beginning thanks to what Christ has done for us. So, if you are having a tough time, remember tomorrow is another day and with Christ you have a new beginning.

John 3:16 is the cornerstone of what we believe: "For God so loved the world that he gave his one and only Son, that whoever believes in him shall not perish but have eternal life." As police officers, we try to help a shattered world. It is comforting to study the words of Jesus. Our hope for eternal life is in this verse. God exemplified the purest form of love known to man by giving up his one and only Son. The road to eternal life is based on our faith in the Father, our belief in his Son, and our willingness to denounce sin in our lives. Our badge will not save us. Our gun will not save us. Only Jesus can save us.

Jesus declared, "I tell you the truth, unless a man is born again, he cannot see the Kingdom of God" (John 3:3). Law enforcement is a career where mortality is a real issue. Nothing is as sad as the funeral of a law enforcement officer killed in the line of duty. It is a tragedy. We must all face the fact that we will someday be separated from this world. Jesus has laid out the plan for eternal life. All we have to do is follow it. John 3:3 lays out a basic part of God's plan: if you want to enter the Kingdom of God, you must be born again.

Are we ready to listen? Are we ready to follow? Jesus offers us his way, the perfect way: "I am the way and the truth and the life. No one comes to the Father except through me" (John 14:6). He is the Author of Truth. When the world around us is searching for answers, we should point them to John 14:6. Better still, we should be a model of truth by allowing others to see Jesus in us.

CHAPTER REFLECTIONS

- Do not worry about today. The Lord is in control.
- Be a lover of the light, not darkness.
- Jesus is the straight and narrow path.
- Rich or poor, God is our Creator.
- Mind your own business.
- We live by faith, not by sight.
- Put your trust in our Savior.
- You must be born again.
- Truth is our goal.
- Jesus is the truth.
- Jesus is the way and the life.

PRAYER FOR THE WAY

Lord, allow me to do things your way. Allow me to stay within your guidelines and boundaries. Show me the way to do everything in your Spirit. Let me show light in a darkened world.

Let me understand the power of heavenly rewards. Make me strong in your word. Let me help those in need of help. Amen.

CHAPTER 8
THE LAW

For police officers, the law is the foundation of our profession. We are sworn to uphold it and required to enforce it. It is at the core of everything we do. The laws of man are complicated. We have thousands of laws designed to make our society a better place to live. But in this chapter, we will focus on God's law. A number of modern-day laws have been passed down through the ages, but only one set comes from God: the Ten Commandments recorded in Exodus 20.

Even in the time of Moses, it was important that people had a standard to live by. God understood this problem and gave Moses the Law that God's people should follow. These Ten Commandments are the sum of all the other laws of our society combined. They seem simple, but when reviewed, we see they are designed to make our life more satisfying.

"You shall have no other Gods before me" (Ex. 20:3).

God wants to be the only God in our lives. He doesn't want us to worship money, career, or other people. He requests that we allow him to be the chief of our hearts and minds. In our modern society, this task has become more difficult as we see those around us so easily swayed to focus their attention on worldly objects and pleasure, but true success happens when we put God first.

Today, we have plenty of alternative gods. We live in a world where success is measured in the things you own. Many law enforcement officers work three and four jobs, not because they need the money but because they *want* material possessions. Their god has become the god of material wealth. Everything they do is enveloped in the desire to acquire more possessions. Some officers become so committed to their extra jobs that they neglect their real job. To them, the side jobs come first, and their regular duty is no longer important. Even their God, families, and friends come second to making money.

Nothing is more important than your God. Look where you spend your time and your energies; that is where you will find your god. If work is always first, that is where your god is. If making money or indulging in hobbies takes priority, your god dwells there. We should daily access where our God lives. If it's not in the Kingdom of Heaven, we should reassess our priorities.

> *"You shall not make for yourself an idol in the form of anything in heaven above or on the earth beneath or in the waters below" (Ex. 20:4).*

Do you have any idols in your life, people or things you idolize? One of America's biggest problems is who we, as a society, choose to be our role models. If you read a list of the most admired people in our country, you will see athletes, movie stars, and musicians. While nothing is wrong with these things, we ask, is that all there is to our society? An idol is something you worship and look to for guidance or direction. Is the guidance these individuals give appropriate? Would you want your children to follow their lead?

It is important to emulate people who are giving proper guidance. However, we need to have Jesus as our example. We should not use individuals, no matter how much we like them, as our standard.

Neither should we make material things our idols. Many believe a new car, money, or boats will bring them happiness. Time and time again, these people are disappointed. Idols are not to be worshipped. The living God is.

"You shall not misuse the name of the Lord your God, for the Lord will not hold anyone guiltless who misuses his name" (Ex. 20:7).

A person's convictions are evidenced by the words they speak. There is a saying, "Strong and bitter words indicate a weak cause." Those people who have to swear and curse every other word provide us with a clear picture of their character. One of the greatest problems we face as a nation is that we don't know how to communicate. Swearing and taking God's name in vain is not effective communication; it's performing. It is someone saying, "Please notice me." We should all strive to be recognized, not by our lips but by our actions.

The irreverence toward God in this kind of language cannot be underestimated. We say *God* and *Jesus* like they mean nothing. When the names of the living God are reduced to swear words, it causes everyone to forget how important these names are. They should be revered and respected. The names of the living God should not be taken lightly.

"Remember the Sabbath day by keeping it holy" (Ex. 20:8).

During the creation period, God took a rest day from all his work. The day of rest was made to offer us a time of relaxation and reflection. By God's example, a man is to labor for six days and rest on the seventh, but the pace of modern-day society has destroyed this plan. Many work seven days a week all year and never take time to pause and rest. We need to examine our priorities in life and set aside time to reflect and worship the Creator. God knows when our occupation demands Sunday hours, but we still must take time to worship and reflect.

We must set apart a day to stop what we are doing and give the day to Jesus. God knows what is best for us. Over and over, we read reports about how Americans are over-worked and stressed out. People have become so busy with living that they have forgotten how to live. Sometimes, we have to pause and reflect on what the cross means to the badge. We have to worship with our families and remember there is more to life than material needs. A day of rest assures we do that. Never forget to rest and meditate on the Lord.

"Honor your father and your mother, so that you may live long in the land the Lord your God is giving you" (Ex. 20:12).

The rise of juvenile crime in America is a major concern. Experts continue to study possible causes for this increase. One cause is the lack of respect in our younger population. In many families, no adult role model is training children in respect. Instead, seven- or eight-year-olds are the adults of the house, raising themselves and their siblings.

These surrogate caregivers are not respected, and they don't give respect to their parents. If these young people do not respect their parents, can we expect them to respect any other adult? Is a child going to respect his teacher if he doesn't respect his mother or father? More times than not, the answer is no.

When this behavior is witnessed, even children from supportive homes question respect. Add to this a youth culture where young people are sold rebellion every day on TV and in music and you can see where the problems begin. God says to honor your parents, and this lesson is taught in the home. If a young person has not been taught to respect their parents, how can they respect themselves? If they do not respect themselves, how will they respect anything?

"You shall not murder" (Ex. 20:13).

How can our country be so advanced in so many key areas yet have the highest murder rate in the free world? While I realize murder is not new, the rate at which it occurs is alarming. America has lost the true value of life as evidenced by our national homicide rate. As a nation, we need to be more sensitive to the victims of violent deaths and their families. Media attention on violence has certainly diminished the personal side of these tragedies. Every murder in this country touches the lives of family and friends who are left to deal with the tragic loss, yet we rarely see that aspect portrayed on the news. We must learn and model the proper way to solve our conflicts without violence.

We should not glorify violence. Every day in our homes we invite violence into our living rooms through our TVs. People who would not dream of allowing their children to see nudity will allow them to watch hours of violence. Violence is not an answer. It destroys lives and murders our young. We should show the same passion for ending senseless violence as we do for preventing our young people from hearing bad language. Violence is almost a tolerated act. We need to rethink our position.

"You shall not commit adultery" (Ex. 20:14).

The toughest call you will ever handle in police work is the domestic call. The emotional bond that exists between a man and a woman, especially if they are married, is strong and passionate, creating an environment ripe for explosive disputes. Marriage is not to be taken lightly. It is a relationship ordained by God. But today, the commitment to marriage is lacking. Men and women take their vows before God and man lightly. God is serious about marriage and the commitment it brings. He is also serious about adultery. Our society, with its fast pace and lack of morals, is tough on the institution of marriage. Marriage takes a great deal of sacrifice and commitment, but it is worth it. Life is better with a loving partner.

In our job, we will encounter people of the opposite sex who are infatuated with us because of our status. We need to be on guard for such advances because the mistakes we make cannot be erased. The hurt and pain an affair can cause is undeniable. Families have been destroyed and lives altered forever because of adultery. How many adults are still damaged by the decisions their parents made when they broke their marriage vows? Before you do anything in a moment of temptation, ask yourself, is it worth destroying my partner or my children? If you think carefully, you will understand the answer is no.

"You shall not steal" (Ex. 20:15).

Have you ever had an item of value stolen from you? It is an empty feeling to return to your car and find several valuable items removed by thieves. While the crime of property theft costs Americans millions of dollars every day, it goes well beyond actual removal of one's property. What about those who defraud insurance companies or those who cheat on their taxes? The people in these two situations may not believe that they are stealing, but what else can you call it? Stealing is wrong, and it is a sin before God, regardless of the way it is carried out.

Stealing also underscores another problem: greed. It is obvious in God's Word that the desire for material things is the root of all evil (1 Tim. 6:10). Greed and envy can cause us to forget God's promise to provide for our needs. What belongs to others should not be tampered with.

"You shall not give false testimony against your neighbor" (Ex. 20:16).

This commandment is the central rule that serves as the cornerstone of our profession. Our justice system is based on the ability of responsible citizens to tell the truth, the whole truth, and nothing but the truth. The system is only as good as the individual credibility of the people involved in it. A sad commentary on our society is the fact that many individuals choose to lie under oath. To give false testimony is a crime called perjury. But, more important, giving false testimony is defined as sin in the Bible. Our sworn duty is to establish and encourage truth. Under God's calling, it becomes the sworn duty of all mankind.

Lies have destroyed more than one person's life. Gossip and deceit are diseases. They start small but eventually consume everything in their path. They cause more hate and discontent in the workplace than any other act. People should learn to stay quiet. Spreading lies and gossip is not only destructive but also a sin.

"You shall not covet your neighbor's house" (Ex. 20:17).

Again, God chooses to return to the theme of greed. Have you ever contemplated how many times avarice is mentioned in the Bible? It is obvious that this condition is sinful. It is the beginning of the end for many people. Greed creates jealousy, anger, deceit, and lies. It is a destroyer.

Are we free of greed? Have we stored our treasures in heaven? Have we run the race like we are going to get the prize? After reading so much about greed and the love of money, it is easy to see why Jesus said, "It is easier for a camel to go through the eye of a needle than for a rich man to enter the kingdom of heaven" (Matt. 19:24).

The Ten Commandments are rules we can and should live by. They are the foundation of the good life in Christ. But it is not enough to know the commandments; we must live them out. And never forget to love the Lawgiver more than the law.

CHAPTER REFLECTIONS

- God wants first place.
- Human idols equal failure.
- Strong and bitter words indicate a weak cause.
- Take time to be holy.
- Honoring our parents is not a choice. It is a commandment.
- You shall not murder.
- Marriage is the core of a moral society.
- You shall not steal.
- Our calling is truth.
- Greed is the root of all evil.

PRAYER FOR THE LAW

God, help me to place you at the top of my priority list. Guide me into recognizing that you deserve first place in my heart and life. Help me to put away thoughts or earthly idols and focus on you. Allow me to speak in a way that's honorable to you. Make me an example of how you would have us to speak. Help me to take time in my busy schedule to acknowledge and worship you.

Thank you for parents and help our young to learn the value of honoring them. Heal our nation from its fascination with homicide and help the victims of these events. Give me the strength to be satisfied with what has been provided and teach me to obtain my wealth honestly. Protect me from false testimony and guide me to use truth as a road to justice. Amen.

CHAPTER 9
OF GOD AND MAN: THE TRIALS OF LIFE

Our faith is often strongest when we are at our lowest ebb. Belief is necessary to sustain us. People are creatures of faith and belief. However, belief is removed from many of us at an early age, and substitutes are added. We are taught to rely on science and logic. We are told that everything has an explanation. We are never told that even science is a guess, at best, and that it is ever growing and changing. Yet, no one would expect a classroom in the twenty-first century to use a science book from the 1940s because the information would be outdated and, in some cases, wrong.

Most of us grew up in a world where we were taught that dinosaurs were the great "Thunder Lizards." Now, we are being told that many dinosaurs are more similar to birds than reptiles in their skeletal structure. And it is possible that we may learn in our lifetime that dinosaurs were birds. Would that make everything we learned in science class incorrect?

How many times have people said that dinosaurs prove that the Judeo-Christian Bible is incorrect? I wonder what people who believed that science was the end of religion must think when their beliefs are shaken. What other things has science been wrong about?

Many people will say that they do not believe in God because they enjoy the reaction they receive. They wear their disbelief on their sleeves like an intellectual badge of honor. They are trapped in a turn-of-the-twentieth-century mentality that states, "I am wise because I know there is no God." Others claim that they cannot believe in God because they believe in science. It appears as if they believe that if they have a degree, they can no longer listen to a voice inside of themselves.

The number of times people say, "Only the unlearned believe in God," is staggering. It seems that any time spirituality is brought up in a conversation, someone in the crowd gives the "I am too smart for God" reaction. These individuals believe that wisdom is a concept you can demonstrate by denying a belief in God. Belief has never had anything to do with human knowledge. Belief means that a person has faith in the impossible. Faith means that a person can believe in things not obvious to the human senses.

Sometimes even religion makes God smaller than he actually is by reducing his complexity to a few rules and regulations. The living God is bigger than rules and tradition.

In one sense, it is obvious that any discussion about God would have to be of the spiritual nature. However, it appears, in many religious settings, that the authorities in charge would rather talk about history and law than the overall power of God. Law and tradition have become more important than the majesty of God.

Surely, there is more to God than remembering a few traditional songs and knowing when to stand up and sit down. If God is the Creator, and surely he is the Creator of all, wouldn't he want to communicate with us?

We can't say we know all there is to know about God, but we should know that God exists. We should know God is here with us personally and in nature and that there is more to life than the physical world of the five senses.

We cheapen God when we attempt to turn the God of all into a scientific theory. Many pseudo-religious leaders need to make God a mathematical problem. This is absurd. The deist wants to explain God as a mythical watchmaker, a great craftsman who has completed his project and watches the results, uninterested in the details. Even in many of today's churches that claim to be spiritual, the

God they worship is lifeless. He has no more miracles to give.

In some Christian circles, the desire to have creation taught as pure science is the goal of many believers. Is that necessary? It is important that we understand how the world was created. However, it is more important to understand why. The understanding of why explains existence. Whether the world was created in seven days or a million years is not as important as why the world was created.

Since we know there is a God, it would be easy to surmise that God is bigger than all knowledge. All knowledge (known, forgotten, and as of yet unlearned) is from God and the sum of the parts is never greater than the whole. If God could be explained and shown in a math problem or a science experiment, it would prove there is no God. There can be no God if he can be explained in simple terms by those less than him. That would make him part of our equation, instead of us being part of his. God would be our creation.

The skeptical mind questions, "Why would God want to speak or communicate with or even acknowledge anything as insignificant as the human race?" We are dirty people, full of all sorts of vices and evil. We love and hate without always being able to explain why.

For every good thing accomplished by the human race, it would be easier to list all of our shortcomings, the lies, the hate, and the sins that reside in every man's heart. Any individual can see it every day. Just turn on the TV and there, in living Technicolor, are all our pride and problems laid bare, like a never-ending episode of reality TV, and we eat it up.

It is true. The human condition is not always nice; it just *is*. And God understands this problem. Greater forces are at play than just science and religion. The Spirit of God is all around, has always lived, and always will be. Spirituality is a feeling, not a concrete experience that can be understood through the five senses. Therefore, emotions are paramount when discussing the spiritual. Let's remove the wall between logic and emotion. The two components should work together to unveil the possibilities of the spiritual life. Logic is important, but emotion should not be forgotten.

Today, many people cut off their understanding of the real world. Their world is limited to their own worldly neighborhood. They have not experienced the world that exists outside the material world. They have not seen the glory beyond the veil.

Every culture that has ever existed has some type of belief in a greater being. Can we be so simple as to write it off as superstition? Is it intellectual superiority that would have the modern man believe every culture before us was not as intelligent as we are?

Spirituality is often ignored, even in the religious community. However, spirituality is the core of our faith. It is the foundation that allows an individual to have the power to see the unseen, hear what is inaudible, and feel what cannot be touched. In brief, it is what makes God, God.

Are we so culturally smug as to believe that everyone before us was ignorant? They had math and science and understood the stars and seasons. They created language and all the forms of communication that we take for granted. These so-called "primitives" created an alphabet and writing. They were not ignorant and unlearned.

God has existed since forever. God will exist for forever. Regardless of what the skeptics say, God will always be worshipped, even when the elite state there is no God. The persistence of worship is the greatest reason I know that there is a God. Neither science nor philosophy nor humanism nor religion will ever replace man's need to know God. And God doesn't need science or religion to explain that need.

We know God by faith. We look past the skeptics and see the truth. We must stay committed to our belief. Often, that belief is shaken when we face hard times. We feel we have been abandoned by God. We feel that a real and benevolent God could not exist and allow these things to happen.

Unfortunately, many bad things that happen are caused by the sin of man. It is not that God does not care;

it is that man does not care. The recklessness of sin affects even the God-fearing. Countless godly men and women have watched as their children chose a path of destruction. That did not happen because God did not care. It happened because he has given people free will.

During hard times, it is easy to get lost and become angry. It is easy to blame God. One of the greatest stories of faith is the story of Job. Through the tribulations of his life, he struggled with his faith and with understanding God. Like us, he heard the calls of an unbelieving world as he faced his problems. He chose to believe in God when his material senses stated that he should abandon hope. Through it all, he remained faithful.

His story is one that brings us strength, yet it focuses on humility. Job was a good person who fell into a test that brought him to his knees. He lost everything but his central hope. Even while totally afflicted with illness and tragedy, he focused his heart on God. Job cried, "Naked I came from my mother's womb, and naked I will depart. The Lord gave and the Lord has taken away; may the name of the Lord be praised" (Job 1:21). If we lost everything we had worked for, could we show the same faith?

Life brings us many challenges. While it is fine to ask why, it is important to direct our questions to the Author of Life, God himself. Job found out through his turmoil that correction, even if from God, can come with a price. While God is the true Author of Life, he certainly does not promise that our existence will be without trouble. As Christians, we frequently witness the trials of life. Many of the trials people experience are the result of bad choices. At times, it would be easy to question God's presence. But it is important to know that God is near.

Job said, "Blessed is the man whom God corrects: so, do not despise the discipline of the Almighty" (Job 5:17). Job was admitting that God's discipline is sometimes tough. Often, as Christians, we want to believe that we are above God's discipline. However, when we move from God's will, we are open to his correction. God is our Abba, our loving Father. What loving father would allow his children to continue doing what is wrong or dangerous? Not only would he be not loving but he would also be neglectful.

During difficult times, people may lose patience. Job must have felt impatient during his time of trouble and turmoil. In our darkest hours, we might wonder, "Is God really there?" If the response is not immediate or in a way we had planned, we question God. Even though it is hard to understand, God is in control. But we must remember his way may not be our way. Remember to be patient and let God work on his schedule, not ours. The Master is in charge of the master schedule. Job understood this and said, "He performs wonders that cannot be fathomed, miracles that cannot be numbered" (Job 9:10).

Job, through all of his hardships, continued to focus on God, even though he felt abandoned. An average person would look at Job's example as one of extremes. Many would say that he was treated unjustly by God. But God is the Author of Justice as Job 9:19 points out: "If it is a matter of strength, he is mighty! And if it is a matter of justice, who will summon him?" During trials, we are often quick to point to God as the source of our misfortunes. But what must be frustrating for God is that when things are good, we seldom give God the praise and the glory.

During his time of trial, Job cried out to God to both voice complaints and ask for mercy. God does not intend for us to take everything in life without question. It is human to question life's turning events. Where we get into trouble is when we question God's ability to get us through them. When Job questioned and complained to God about his turmoil, he was presented a short response about God's great power. The Lord spoke to Job and informed him, in so many words, that he controls the past, present and future. God asked, "Have you ever given orders to the morning?" (Job 38:12). What a statement of God's great power to guide us in the midst of trouble! If you are facing a difficult time in life, turn to the one who created the morning, instead of cursing him.

During life's toughest moments, nothing is as comforting as Psalm 23: "The Lord is my shepherd, I shall lack nothing." This passage of scripture has been recited during countless tragedies. The obstacles we face each day become smaller when we read the powerful words of this popular scripture. As law enforcement officers, we like to rely on our own strength and courage. But as humans we must face the fact that there are situations where we would fail by our power alone. Take time today to read through the twenty-third Psalm. It will lead you to a higher level of personal and professional confidence.

God does care, even in difficult times. Anyone who has lost a loved one tragically understands the heartache of sorrow. God does care. He loves you when you are suffering and wants to comfort you. And even after death, he loves those who love him and welcomes them into his kingdom.

CHAPTER REFLECTIONS

- The Lord gives, and the Lord takes away.
- Blessed is the man God corrects.
- Mankind needs the great physician.
- Sometimes miracles hide.
- Who will summon God?
- Have faith in God alone.
- God is the loving Father.
- God welcomes questions because he has the answers.
- The great Creator can create a new beginning for you.
- The Lord is my shepherd.

PRAYER FOR OUR TRIALS

Lord, in the midst of sickness and sorrow, please draw near so I may see your face and experience your peace. Thank you for your presence in the trials of life and for your many blessings each day. When times are tough, teach me to depend on your strength and guidance to get me through. Even though at times you may be silent, thank you for your hidden miracles.

Teach me to accept reality and help me to lift up praise to you during the good times as well as the bad. Hear my questions and complaints and calm my fears and doubts. Thank you for your great power and wisdom. Help me to focus my attention on you and your promises. Thank you for green pastures and for sharing them. Amen.

CHAPTER 10

THE RESURRECTION OF JESUS TIMES FOUR

No greater story than the resurrection of Jesus Christ has ever been told. It is the story that means the most to Christians because it tells of a wonderful redeemer who loved mankind enough to die for us.

We hope that while you have read this book you've reflected on the grace and love Jesus has for you. The resurrection shows the power of Jesus and his love for each of us. The following is a recreation of the Easter Story. It is based on all four gospels of the King James version of the Bible. It is not a complete recreation, and we realize you may even have your own ideas about the first Easter. We are not here to change your mind. We just want to share the glory of our risen Lord:

And when the Sabbath was past, Mary Magdalene, and Joanna, and Mary, the mother of James and Salome, bought sweet spices, that they might come and anoint Jesus. They came to the tomb at the rising of the sun. And, behold, there was a great earthquake, for the angel of the Lord descended from heaven, and came and rolled back the stone from the door, and sat upon it. His countenance was like lightning, and his garments white as snow. And for fear of him, the keepers did shake, and become as dead men.

Before the women arrived, they had asked themselves, "Who will roll away the stone from the door of the tomb?" But, when they arrived, the stone had already been removed. The women entered the tomb and did not find the body of the Lord Jesus. Then, Mary Magdalene ran, and came to Simon Peter, and to John, the other disciple, whom Jesus loved, and said to them, "They have taken away the Lord out of the tomb, and we know not where they have laid him."

Peter and John went to the tomb. They ran together, and John ran past Peter and came first to the tomb. As John knelt down, and looked in, he saw the linen clothes lying folded inside, but he did not go in.

Then came Simon Peter following him, and he went into the tomb, and saw that the linen clothes were empty. The napkin that was about his head was not lying with the linen clothes, but was wrapped together in a place by itself. John then entered, and he saw and believed.

Then, the disciples went away again to their own home. But Mary and the other women stood outside the tomb weeping. As Mary Magdalene wept, she stooped down, and looked into the tomb. She saw two angels in white sitting to the right of the linen, one at the head, and the other at the feet, where the body of Jesus had lain. The other women looked in and were perplexed.

And one of the angels said to Mary Magdalene, "Woman, why do you weep?" She replied, "Because they have taken away my Lord, and I know not where they have laid him." The women were afraid and bowed down their heads to the earth. The angels asked Mary Magdalene, "Why seek the living among the dead? He is not here, but is risen. Remember how he spoke to you when he was yet in Galilee, saying the Son of Man must be delivered into the hands of sinful men, and be crucified, and, on the third day rise, again." And the women remembered Jesus' words.

The angel said, "Be not afraid. You seek Jesus of Nazareth, which was crucified. He is risen; he is not here. Behold the place where they laid him. Go your way, tell his disciples and Peter that he goes before you into Galilee. There you will see him, as he told you." The women went out quickly and fled from the tomb. They trembled as they left, and were amazed. They did not say anything to any man.

And as they left, they saw Jesus, but they did not know it was Him. Jesus said, "Woman, why do you weep? Who do you seek?" Mary Magdalene, thinking he was the gardener, said, "Sir, if you have moved him, tell me where you have laid him, and I will take him away." Jesus replied, "Mary." She turned and said to him, "Rabboni," which is to say, "Master."

Jesus said, "All hail." And they came and held him by the feet and worshipped him. Jesus said to them, "Touch me not; for I am not yet ascended to my Father, but go to my brethren, and say unto them, I have ascended to my Father, and your Father; and to my God, and your God." Then, Jesus said, "Be not afraid. Go tell my brethren to go into Galilee, and there shall they see me."

Now, while they were going, some of the watch came into the city and showed the chief priests all the things that were done. And when the chief priests were assembled with the elders, and had taken counsel, they gave large amounts of money to the soldiers to say his disciples came by night and stole him away while they slept.

Two other followers left that same day for a village called Emmaus, which was about seven miles from Jerusalem. They were talking about all the events which had happened. And it came to pass, that, while they talked together and reasoned, Jesus himself drew near, and went with them. But their eyes were closed, so that they should not know him. And Jesus said, "What are you talking about?" The two travelers stopped and looked sad.

One of the followers, Cleopas, answered, "Are you a stranger in Jerusalem? Do you not know the things which have come to pass in these days?" Jesus answered, "What things?" And they said to him, "Concerning Jesus of Nazareth, who was a prophet mighty in deed and word before God and all the people. You don't know how the chief priests and our rulers delivered him to be condemned to death and crucified him. We trusted that it had been him which should have redeemed Israel and beside all this, today is the third day since these things were done."

The followers continued their discussion with Jesus. "Yes, and certain women of our company astonished us. They went to the tomb early and when they did not find his body, they came, saying, that they had also seen a vision of angels, which said that he *was alive. And certain of them which were with us went to the tomb and found it even so as the women had said."*

Then, Jesus said to them, "O fools, and slow of heart to believe all that the prophets have spoken. Ought not Christ to have suffered these things and to enter into his glory?" And beginning at Moses and all the prophets, he expounded to them in all the Scriptures the things concerning himself.

The followers went to the village, and Jesus made as though he would have gone further. But they stopped him, saying, "Abide with us, for it is toward evening, and the day is far spent." And Jesus went in, to tarry with them. And it came to pass, as he sat at dinner with them, he took bread, and blessed it, and gave it to them.

And their eyes were opened, and they knew him; and he vanished out of their sight. And they said, one to another, "Did not our hearts burn within us, while he talked with us by the way, and while he opened to us the Scriptures?"

They rose up the same hour and returned to Jerusalem and found the eleven gathered together. As they told their story, the eleven shouted, "The Lord has risen indeed and has appeared to Simon." And the followers told what things had been done and how Jesus was known to them in the breaking of the bread.

That same evening, when the doors were shut where the disciples were assembled for fear of the Jews, Jesus came and stood in their midst, and said to them, "Peace be unto you." And when he had said this, he breathed on them, and said to them, "Receive the Holy Ghost."

But they were terrified and surmised that they had seen a spirit. And he said to them, "Why are you troubled? Why do thoughts arise in your hearts? Behold my hands and my feet. It is me. Handle me and see; for a spirit has not flesh and bones." When he said this, he showed them his hands and his feet.

The disciples stood in disbelief. Jesus said, "Have you any food?" And they gave him a piece of a broiled fish and a honeycomb. And he took it and ate before them. And he said, "These are the words which I spoke to you, while I was with you, that all things must be fulfilled, which were written in the law of Moses, and in the prophets, and in the Psalms, concerning me."

This opened their understanding, that they might understand the Scriptures. Jesus said, "That it is written, and thus it was necessary for Christ to suffer, and to rise from the dead on the third day. And that repentance and remission of sins should be preached in his name among all nations, beginning at Jerusalem. And, behold, I send the promise of my Father upon you, but tarry in the city of Jerusalem, until you are provided with the power from on high."

Thomas, one of the twelve, called Didymus, was not with them when Jesus came. The other disciples therefore said to him, "We have seen the Lord." But Thomas replied, "Except I shall see in his hands the print of the nails and put my finger into the print of the nails, and thrust my hand into his side, I will not believe."

After eight days, again his disciples were within, and Thomas was with them. Then came Jesus, the doors being shut, and stood in the midst, and said, "Peace be unto you." Then, Jesus said to Thomas, "Reach hither thy finger and behold my hands; and reach hither thy hand, and thrust it into my side: and be not faithless, but believing."

Thomas answered and said to him, "My Lord and my God." Jesus said, "Thomas, because you have seen me, you have believed. Blessed are they that have not seen and yet have believed."

Jesus showed himself again to the disciples at the sea of Tiberias. Together were Simon Peter, and Thomas called Didymus, and Nathanael of Cana in Galilee, and the sons of Zebedee, and two other disciples. Simon Peter said, "I am going fishing." The others replied, "We will also go." They went forth and entered into a ship immediately, and that night, they caught nothing. But when the morning came, Jesus stood on the shore. The disciples did not know it was Jesus. Then, Jesus said, "Children, have you any fish?" They answered him, "No."

Jesus told them, "Cast the net on the right side of the ship." They threw their nets and now they were not able to draw it in for the multitude of fishes. Therefore, that disciple whom Jesus loved said to Peter, "It is the Lord."

Now, when Simon Peter heard that it was the Lord, he put his clothes on, (for he was naked) and threw himself into the sea. And the other disciples came in a little ship, dragging the net with fishes. As soon then as they came to land, they saw a fire of coals cooking fish and bread.

Jesus said, "Bring the fish which you caught." Simon Peter went up and drew the net to the land. It was full of great fishes, a hundred and fifty-three. There were so many fish, yet the net had not broken. Jesus said, "Come and dine." And none of the disciples asked, "Who are you?," knowing that it was the Lord.

Jesus then came and took the bread and fish and gave it to them. This was now the third time that Jesus showed himself to his disciples, after he was risen from the dead. So, when they had dined, Jesus said to Simon Peter, "Simon, son of John, do you love me more than these?" Simon Peter answered, Yes, Lord; you know that I love you." Jesus replied, "Feed my lambs."

Jesus asked again, "Simon, son of John, do you love me?" Simon Peter answered, "Yes, Lord; you know that I love you." Jesus said to him, "Feed my sheep."

A third time Jesus asked, "Simon, son of John, do you love me?" Simon Peter was grieved because he said it to him the third time, and he said to him, "Lord, you know all things; you know that I love you." Jesus said to him, "Feed my sheep."

Jesus continued, as Simon Peter listened, "Verily, verily, I say unto you, 'When you were young, you guided yourself, and walked where you wanted, but when you are old, you shall stretch forth your hands, and another shall guide you, and carry you where you do not want to go.'"

Simon Peter asked what death would glorify God. And Jesus answered, "Follow me." Then Peter, turning about, saw the disciple whom Jesus loved and said, "Lord, what shall this man do?" Jesus said, "If it is my will, he will tarry till I come. What is that to you?" Then went this saying abroad among the brethren, that John should not die, yet Jesus did not say that. He said, "If it is my will, he will tarry till I come. What is that to you?"

Later, the eleven disciples went away into Galilee, into a mountain where Jesus had appointed them. Jesus appeared to the eleven as they sat at dinner and counseled them for their unbelief and hardness of heart, because they believed not them which had seen him after he was risen. And he said to them, "Go into all the world and preach the Gospel to every creature. He that believes and is baptized shall be saved, but he that believes not shall be damned. And these signs shall follow them that believe; in my name shall they cast out devils, they shall speak with new tongues, they shall take up serpents, and if they drink any deadly thing, it shall not hurt them; they shall lay hands on the sick and they shall recover. All power is given unto me in heaven and in earth. Go therefore, and teach all nations, baptizing them in the name of the Father, and of the Son, and of the Holy Ghost. Teaching them to observe all things whatsoever, I have commanded you: and, lo, I am with you always, even unto the end of the world."

So then, after the Lord had spoken to them, he was received up into heaven and sat on the right hand of God. And they went forth and preached everywhere, the Lord working with them, and confirming the word with signs following. And there are also many other things which Jesus did, if they should be

*written every one, I suppose that even the world itself
could not contain the books that should be written.*

Jesus's death and resurrection is the greatest story ever told. It should never be forgotten. In our day-to-day lives, it is easy to forget that Jesus should be put first. We, as Christians, cannot afford to forget this story of resurrection power.

We have spent many chapters discussing our roles as Christians and police officers. We should never forget that we are Christians first. Christ is our savior and our redeemer. Nothing should stand in our way of serving the Lord. He is risen. He is risen, indeed.

REPENT FOR THE DAY OF THE LORD IS NEAR

Who is the man who is called the Son of God?
Who is the man who is called the Son of Man?
Repent for the day of the Lord is near.
Sing your songs of praise—worthy is the Lamb.
Hosanna, Hosanna,
Worship the Almighty God.
—JBS

ABOUT THE AUTHOR

BOBBY KIPPER

Bobby Kipper is a *Wall Street Journal* and *USA Today* bestselling author. He started his thirty-year law enforcement career with the Newport News Police Department (Virginia) before becoming the executive director of Virginia's Gang Reduction Program at the office of the attorney general. Bobby currently serves as the founder and executive director of the National Center for Prevention of Community Violence (NCPCV).

During his three decades of law enforcement service, he discovered a void in spiritual wellness for police officers, which led him to journaling his own thoughts on navigating the constant negative impact that daily police duty can have on one's perspective of people and life.

Roll Call is the byproduct of those thoughts and is dedicated to the men and women, past and present, who have made and continue to make our communities safe.

A free ebook edition is available with the purchase of this book.

To claim your free ebook edition:

1. Visit MorganJamesBOGO.com
2. Sign your name CLEARLY in the space
3. Complete the form and submit a photo of the entire copyright page
4. You or your friend can download the ebook to your preferred device

Morgan James BOGO™

A **FREE** ebook edition is available for you or a friend with the purchase of this print book.

_____

CLEARLY SIGN YOUR NAME ABOVE

Instructions to claim your free ebook edition:
1. Visit MorganJamesBOGO.com
2. Sign your name CLEARLY in the space above
3. Complete the form and submit a photo of this entire page
4. You or your friend can download the ebook to your preferred device

Print & Digital Together Forever.

Snap a photo

Free ebook

Read anywhere